THE
DILBERT™
FUTURE

THE
DILBERT™
FUTURE

Thriving on Stupidity in
the 21st Century

SCOTT ADAMS

HarperBusiness
A Division of HarperCollinsPublishers

HarperCollins books may be purchased for educational, business, or sales promotional use. For information please write: Special Markets Department, HarperCollins Publishers, Inc., 10 East 53rd Street, New York, NY 10022.

FIRST EDITION

Designed by Nancy Singer

Library of Congress Cataloging-in-Publication Data

Adams, Scott, 1957–
    The Dilbert future : thriving on stupidity in the 21st
century / by Scott Adams. — 1st ed.
      p.   cm.
   ISBN 0-88730-866-X
   1. American wit and humor. I. Title.
PN6162.A345 1997
741.5'973—dc21   97-7137

97 98 99 00 01 ❖/RRD 10 9 8 7 6 5 4 3 2 1

Dedicated to my parents,
Paul and Virginia Adams,
so they won't be too mad that
I made jokes about them

CONTENTS

INTRODUCTION 1

1 HOW TO PREDICT THE FUTURE 5

Adams's Rule of the Unexpected 5
Adams's Rule of Self-Defeating Prophecies 6
Adams's Rule of Logical Limits 6

2 AGING 9

Retirement 11
Genetically Engineered Children 11
Children Are Our Future .12

3 TECHNOLOGY PREDICTIONS 17

Life Will Not Be Like *Star Trek* 17
Technology to Avoid Work 26
The Future of the Internet 29
Clothing of the Future 31
The Network Computer versus the Personal Computer 33
ISDN 40
The Bozo Filter 46
Censorship on the Internet 50
Technology Makes Us Less Productive 53
Energy Sources 56
Technology as the Leading Cause of Death 58
Men Who Use Computers—The New Sex Symbols 65

4   LIFE ON OTHER PLANETS   71

5   THE WORLD GETS MORE COMPLICATED   75

The Incompetence Line 80
Your Busy Life 89
Household Services 89

6   THE FUTURE OF DEMOCRACY AND CAPITALISM   93

The Future of Voting 96
Vote Deflation 99
The Rise of the Hairy Reasoners 101

7   THE FUTURE OF GENDER RELATIONS   105

Sex in the Future 105
Women in Charge 107
Technology to Free Men 115

8   THE FUTURE OF WORK   119

The Future of Managers 119
Employee Motivation 123
The Revenge of the Downsized 126
The Job Search in the Future 129
Outsourcing .134
The Job Model of the Future 136
The Future of Telecommuting 143
The Future of Office Workstations 149
Acronyms Shortages 155
Industrial Espionage 158

9 MARKETING IN THE FUTURE

Spiderweb Marketing Strategy 166
Markets of the Future 170

10 GOOD AND BAD JOBS OF THE FUTURE

Mothers, Don't Let Your Children Grow Up to Be Vendors. . .178
Procurement 180
Temp 181
Accounting, Auditing, and Dentistry 183
Venture Capitalist 186
Records Retention   .188
Get Paid to Criticize Others 189

11 SOCIAL STUFF

Poverty 191
The Age of Consent 192
Crime 193
News in the Future 199
Parent Licenses 204
Euthanasia 206
Privacy 208
Pet Services 211
Food in the Future   .213

12 ENDANGERED SPECIES

13 SOME THINGS WON'T IMPROVE

Airlines 221
Bicycle Seats 222

14 A NEW VIEW OF THE FUTURE   225

The Double Slit Experiment 231
Objects Move 235
Gravity Exists 236
Cause and Effect 240
Chaos Theory 244
Affirmations 246

APPENDIX A: AFFIRMATIONS TECHNIQUE   255

APPENDIX B: DISCLAIMERS OF ORIGINALITY   257

INTRODUCTION

There are two types of people in the world: the bright and attractive people like yourself who read *Dilbert* books, and the 6 billion idiots who get in our way. Since we're outnumbered, it's a good idea not to refer to them as idiots to their faces. A devious *Dilbert* reader suggested calling them "Induh-viduals" instead. The advantage to this word is that you can insult someone without risk of physical harm. Example:

You: You're quite an Induhvidual, Tim.

Tim: Thank you.

If you're not already surrounded by Induhviduals, you will be soon. New ones are being born every minute, despite the complexity involved in breeding. Frankly, I think much of the procreation of Induhviduals happens purely by accident when two of them are trying to do something complicated—like jump-start a car—and they suddenly get confused. Whatever causes the breeding—and I truly don't want to know the details—it's safe to assume there will be more of it.

The way I see it, you have three good strategies for thriving in a future full of Induhviduals:

1. Wear loose clothing and pretend your car battery is dead.

2. Keep Induhviduals in your car so you can use the car-pool lane.

3. Harness the stupidity of Induhviduals for your own financial gain.

Option one is dangerous. I recommend that you stay away from anything that involves Induhviduals, electricity, and sex. It's just common sense.

Option two requires you to be in your car with Induhviduals for long periods of time. There is a real risk that they will attempt to make conversation. That would negate any benefits you get from avoiding traffic congestion. And if you accidentally leave them in the car and forget to crack the window open, they'll die. You'll need more than one of those little Christmas-tree air fresheners to solve that problem.

I recommend option three: Harness the stupidity of Induhviduals for your own financial gain. In order to do that, you'll need to be able to anticipate their moves well in advance. This can be difficult, because the average Induhvidual does not anticipate his own moves in advance.

If you asked the average Induhvidual about his plans, he'd say he has no plans. But if you yanked the eight-track tape player out of that Induhvidual's Pinto and then repeatedly hit that average Induhvidual with it, you could make him confess that he has some plans, even if those plans are not very exciting:

Average Induhvidual's Plans

- Become shorter and more crotchety over time.

- Lose all appreciation of popular music.

- Cultivate ear hair.

- Get a new eight-track player.

Clearly, with a world full of people who have goals like that, most of the things that happen in the future will not be the result of good planning. That makes the future difficult to predict. That's why you need this book.

I have compiled my predictions here so you won't have any unpleasant surprises during the next millennium. Any morning you're wondering whether it would be better to drown yourself in your cereal bowl or face 6 billion Induhviduals again, at least you'll be making an informed decision.

This book is an exhaustive analysis of the future, in the sense that if you held the book above your head for several hours, you would become exhausted. I recommend you do just that before reading it so you'll be groggy and won't notice that the paragraphs don't all fit together—like this next one.

I'm more of a sprinter than a marathoner when it comes to many aspects of life. For example, when I'm running. Over short distances—up to two yards—I can run faster than cheap panty hose on an itchy porcupine. But over long distances, I'm not so impressive.

I try to compensate for my lack of long-distance endurance by having good form. I'm told that my running style is quite majestic. That's probably because I learned to run by watching nature films in which leopards chased frightened zebras. Now when I run, I open my eyes real wide and let my tongue slap the side of my face. If you saw it, you'd be saying, "That's very majestic." And then you'd run like a frightened zebra. That's why my homeowners association voted to ask me to do my jogging with a pillowcase over my head.

If you think none of this is relevant to the future, you'd be oh-so-wrong, because it leads quite neatly to my first prediction:

PREDICTION 1

In the future, authors will take a long time to get to the point.
That way the book looks thicker.

There are many methods for predicting the future. For example, you can read horoscopes, tea leaves, tarot cards, or crystal balls. Collectively, these methods are known as "nutty methods." Or you can put well-researched facts into sophisticated computer models, more commonly referred to as "a complete waste of time." While these approaches have their advantages, none are appropriate for this book, because they require more work than sitting in front of my computer and typing. Instead, I will use these far-more-efficient methods to divine the future:

Methods for Divining the Future

1. My awesome powers of logic.

2. My crystal-clear observations.

3. My almost frightening intuition.

4. My total lack of guilt.

The future is an excellent topic for any author. By the time you realize I was wrong about everything I predicted, I will be dead. Business schools refer to that phenomenon as the "time value of money," or more colloquially as "GOOD LUCK GETTING A REFUND NOW!!"

Books about the future also have a nice upside potential. For example, let's say most of civilization is destroyed by some huge calamity. (That's not the good part.) And let's say a copy of this book somehow gets encased in amber and trapped in a tar pit. (It happens more often than you'd think. It happened to my brother. He makes a great conversation piece.) Eons from now, when our descendants find it (the book, not my brother), they will read my predictions and believe I was a wise holy man. I think I'll like that, except for the part about being dead.

As with my previous books, I will say a lot of obvious things that you already agree with, thereby making me look like a genius. But in a departure from the past, I will also say as many controversial and inflammatory things as I can (i.e., pretending to have actual opinions). If lots of gullible Induhviduals get mad at me, it might generate enough publicity to get me invited as a guest on *Larry King Live*. That's really the goal here. So if you see something that makes you mad, don't just sit there, organize a protest. I'll chip in for the poster boards and Magic Markers.

Throughout this book, I will delve into many areas in which I am thoroughly incompetent, including politics, history, economics, physiology, and particle physics. My intellectual shortcomings will manifest themselves as inaccuracies, misconceptions, and logical flaws. I recommend that you read it quickly so you won't notice.

ONE

HOW TO PREDICT THE FUTURE

Some people try to predict the future by assuming current trends will continue. This is a bad method. For example, if you applied that forecasting method to a puppy, you'd predict that the puppy would continue growing larger and larger until one day—in a fit of uncontrolled happiness—its wagging tail would destroy a major metropolitan area. But that rarely happens, thanks to the National Guard.

The future never follows trends, because of three rules I have named after myself in order to puff up my importance.

ADAMS'S RULE OF THE UNEXPECTED

Something unexpected always happens to wreck any good trend. Here are some examples to prove my point:

GOOD TREND	UNEXPECTED BAD THING
Computers allow us to work 100 percent faster.	Computers generate 300 percent more work.
Women get more political power.	Women are as dumb as men.
Popular music continues to get better.	I get old.

ADAMS'S RULE OF SELF-DEFEATING PROPHECIES

Whenever humans notice a bad trend, they try to change it. The prediction of doom causes people to do things differently and avoid the doom. Any doom that can be predicted won't happen.

Here are some examples of dooms that people predicted and how the indomitable human spirit rose to the challenge and thwarted the prediction:

PREDICTION OF DOOM	HUMAN RESPONSE
Population will grow faster than food supply.	Scientists realize you can call just about anything a "meat patty."
Petroleum reserves will be depleted in twenty years.	Scientists discover oil in their own hair.
Communism will spread to the rest of the world.	All Communists become ballerinas and defect.

I might have some of the details wrong; I'm working from memory here. But the point is that none of those predictions came true once we started worrying about them. That's the way it always works.

ADAMS'S RULE OF LOGICAL LIMITS

All trends have logical limits. For example, computers continue to shrink in size, but that trend will stop as soon as you hear this report on CNN:

This just in. A computer systems administrator sneezed, and his spray destroyed the entire military computing hardware of North America, leading to the conquest of the United States by Haitian bellhops. More on that later, but first our report on the healing powers of herbal tea.

At that point, we'll say, "Hey, maybe those computers were too small." That will be the end of the shrinking computer trend.

If all trends end, what can we look at to predict the future? There are some things in life so consistent that they are like immutable laws of human nature. You can predict most of the future by looking at these immutable laws and applying logic.

Immutable Laws of Human Nature

- Stupidity

- Selfishness

- Horniness

Those are the things that will never change, no matter what else does. People don't change their basic nature, they just accumulate more stuff upon which they can apply their stupidity, selfishness, and horniness. From this perspective, the future isn't hard to predict.

I realize that by telling you my secrets I'm not only opening my kimono, but I'm also doing jumping jacks in front of your picture window, if you catch my visual gist. But I'm not worried about you learning my secrets, because I'll always be one step ahead of you.

PREDICTION 2

In the future, you will wish I had never put the image in your head of me doing jumping jacks in an open kimono.

TWO

AGING

Human life expectancies increase every year. This is not necessarily a good thing.

PREDICTION 3

On average, Induhviduals who are alive today will experience 80 years of complaint-free living. Unfortunately, they'll live to 160.

The aging of Induhviduals will create some big challenges for businesses. Senior citizens are never in a hurry, and they're not willing to put up with any crap. The average retail transaction will take up to three days. It won't even be that quick unless stores start accepting as legal tender whatever elderly Induhviduals find in their pockets. Merchants will be forced to accept hard candy, tissues, and bird seed as payment. But that's okay. The merchants will handle it the same way they handle Canadian pennies and Kennedy fifty-cent pieces—by giving them to timid customers as change.

I make fun of senior citizens, but obviously I aspire to be one of them, the alternative being what it is. Unfortunately, not all older people will be pleasant, intelligent, and reasonable—the way I plan to be. Many will be Induhviduals who somehow managed to survive for years without ever eating anything from a container with a skull on it. This means trouble, because the only thing worse than being surrounded by Induhviduals is being surrounded by senior citizen Induhviduals.

Young Induhviduals sometimes feel pressure to keep their thoughts to themselves, but that impulse goes away over time. Eventually, we'll have several billion senior citizen Induhviduals who will feel the need to complain loudly about things they don't understand, which, as you can guess, will include just about everything. The cumulative noise from all that whining will cause planet-wide deafness in small animals.

However, there is a solution. It's called cryogenic freezing. The theory is that when someone has an incurable illness, you can freeze their bodies and then thaw them out in the future when scientists have invented a cure. This seems like a perfect solution, assuming we have enough storage space.

Cryogenic freezing has several advantages:

1. The Induhvidual pays for it himself.

2. Technically, it's not murder.

3. There's no gooey stuff to clean up.

4. You can convince their relatives to kiss them and watch the fun as their lips get frozen stuck.

All you have to do is convince the Induhviduals around you that they have incurable illnesses and cryogenics is their only hope. You'd get the hypochondriacs first. They'd be the easiest. You could get a few million more Induhviduals to sign up for the plan by sending them a computer virus through the Internet. You'd be surprised how many Induhviduals think they can get viruses from their computers.

For the rest of the Induhviduals, you'd need accomplices in the medical community. But I don't think it will be a problem because unlike retailers, doctors won't put up with being paid in hard candy, tissues, and bird seed.

RETIREMENT

Most people are not saving enough money for retirement. If you're one of them, I suggest you start exercising vigorously so that later in life you can bully your frail peers and take their stuff when you need it.

I often see senior citizens in the park practicing Tai Chi Chuan. The *alleged* purpose is to increase balance and energy or some such baloney. What ever happened to TAKING A WALK?

You don't need to learn lethal skills to increase balance and energy. It's obvious to me that those senior citizens are preparing to slap the bejeezus out of the rest of us and take our stuff. They're just biding their time and waiting for us to realize there isn't enough retirement money for everyone.

Many of you are saving money instead of exercising. It seems like a smart thing to do, but later you'll be cursing yourselves as you watch the Tai Chi experts carry your stuff away in huge boxes.

PREDICTION 4

The people who are studying Tai Chi Chuan instead of saving money are planning to beat us up and take our stuff when we're retired.

Don't say I didn't warn you.

GENETICALLY ENGINEERED CHILDREN

At some point—probably in your lifetime—we'll have the technology to make all children tall, lean, and muscular. They'll have smooth skin, perfect hair, good teeth, and 20/20 vision. All genetic abnormalities will be spotted and corrected in the womb. This is very good news for the people born in the future.

It is very bad news for those of you reading this book. We'll look like a hideous Quasimodo society to the perfect generation that will follow us. We'll not only be old, we'll have a whole range of physical imperfections that will make us appear repulsive to the young. They'll look like the cast of *Baywatch* and we'll look like extras on *The X-Files*.

PREDICTION 5

The people who are alive today will appear grotesque to the perfectly engineered children of the future.

This situation will cause an even greater rift between the older and younger generations. But it will also ease our guilt about plundering the planet and leaving our garbage and debt to those ungrateful little Barbie and Ken dolls. So it's not entirely bad.

CHILDREN ARE OUR FUTURE

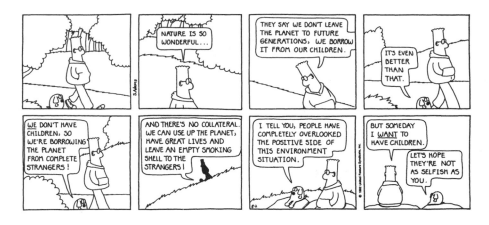

True Story

The scene is a grocery store. A father studies a can of chili. His ten-year-old son stands nearby. His mother is at the far end of the aisle picking up another item. I am one of a dozen other shoppers in this aisle. The father says to his son, "Ask your

mother if Hormel chili is okay." The son turns and yells at the
top of his lungs, "HEY MOM! IS HORMEL CHILI OKAY?!"

The children are our future. And that is why, ultimately, we're screwed
unless we do something about it. If you haven't noticed, the children who
are our future are good-looking, but they aren't all that bright. As dense as
they might be, they will eventually notice that adults have spent all the
money, spread disease, and turned the planet into a smoky, filthy ball of
death. We're raising an entire generation of dumb, pissed-off kids who
know where the handguns are kept. This is not a good recipe for a happy
future.

Fortunately, there's a solution: Brainwashing.

PREDICTION 6

In the future, we will accelerate our successful practice of
brainwashing children so they'll be nice to us while we
plunder their planet.

Brainwashing the children is the only logical solution to our problems.
The alternative is for adults to stop running up debts, polluting, and having
reckless sex. For this to happen, several billion Induhviduals would have to
become less stupid, selfish, and horny. This is not likely.

The path of least resistance is brainwashing the kids. We do it already in
lots of ways and it works well. Obviously, we'll have to use a different word
than "brainwashing." I suggest calling it "lessons in right and wrong," just
as our parents did.

Children's brains are like fresh mashed potatoes that you can push
around with your fork, making a little bowl to hold your gravy. If you get to
them early, you create little citizens who grow up to enthusiastically volun-
teer for amazingly dangerous tasks—such as killing people in other countries.

I know you can't always tell when I'm kidding. So to be perfectly clear:

I'm *totally in favor of brainwashing.* Brainwashing works, which is why there will be a lot more of it in the future.

There are some forms of brainwashing that most of us will agree are good. This will form the baseline requirements for all kids in the future, just as it does today:

Acceptable Brainwashing

- Respect your elders.

- Worship God.

- Democracy is the best system.

- Just say no to drugs.

- Low-paying jobs are "honest work."

- Buy *Dilbert* products.

We'll need to add a few new brainwashing themes to prepare for the future.

Additional Brainwashing

- It is an honor to give your money to old, ugly people.

- It is a privilege to experience the pollution of previous generations.

- Wrinkles are sexy.

- Forgetfulness is a sign of wisdom.

- God likes it when you use all your money to pay interest on your parents' debts.

- Baldness, huge thighs, and potbellies are all signs of intelligence and sexual potency.

Some might say this view of the future is too cynical. They might say adults can learn to change their behavior and reverse the damage they're causing the planet, thus protecting the world for future generations. My response to this argument is, "There's no such thing as being TOO cynical."

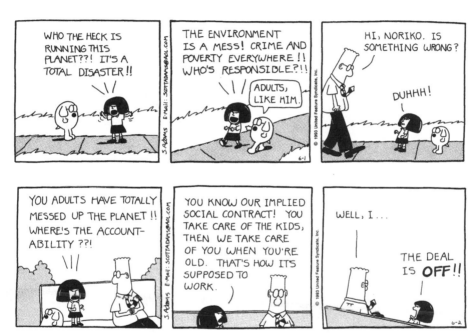

THREE

TECHNOLOGY PREDICTIONS

LIFE WILL NOT BE LIKE *STAR TREK*

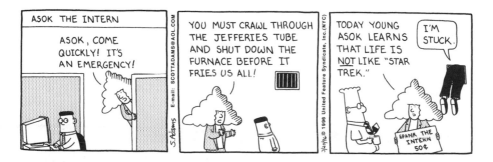

There are so many *Star Trek* spin-offs that it's easy to fool yourself into thinking that the *Star Trek* vision is an accurate vision of the future. Sadly, *Star Trek* does not take into account the stupidity, selfishness, and horniness of the average human being. In this chapter, I will explore some of the flaws in the *Star Trek* vision of the future.

PREDICTION 7

Life in the future will *not* be like *Star Trek*.

Medical Technology

On *Star Trek,* the doctors have handheld devices that instantly close any openings in the skin. Imagine that sort of device in the hands of your unscrupulous friends. They would sneak up behind you and seal your ass shut as a practical joke. The devices would be sold in novelty stores instead of medical outlets. All things considered, I'm happy that it's not easy to close other peoples' orifices.

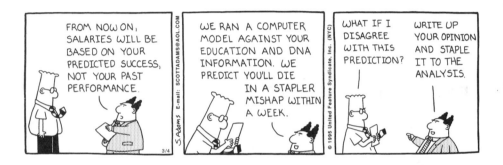

Transporter

It would be great to be able to beam your molecules across space and then reassemble them. The only problem is that you have to trust your co-worker to operate the transporter. These are the same people who won't add paper to the photocopier or make a new pot of coffee after taking the last drop. I don't think they'll be double-checking the transporter coordinates. They'll be accidentally beaming people into walls, pets, and furniture. People will spend all their time apologizing for having inanimate objects protruding from parts of their bodies.

"Pay no attention to the knickknacks; I got beamed into a hutch yesterday."

If I could beam things from one place to another, I'd never leave the house. I'd sit in a big comfy chair and just start beaming groceries, stereo equipment, cheerleaders, and anything else I wanted right into my house. I'm fairly certain I would abuse this power. If anybody came to arrest me, I'd beam them into space. If I wanted some paintings for my walls, I'd beam the contents of the Louvre over to my place, pick out the good stuff, and beam the rest into my neighbor's garage.

If I were watching the news on television and didn't like what I heard, I would beam the anchorman into my living room during the commercial break, give him a vicious wedgie, and beam him back before anybody noticed.

I'd never worry about "keeping up with the Joneses," because as soon as they got something nice, it would disappear right out of their hands. My neighbors would have to use milk crates for furniture. And that's only after I had all the milk crates I would ever need for the rest of my life.

There's only one thing that could keep me from spending all my time wreaking havoc with the transporter: the holodeck.

Holodeck

For those of you who only watched the "old" *Star Trek*, the holodeck can create simulated worlds that look and feel just like the real thing. The characters on *Star Trek* use the holodeck for recreation during breaks from work. This is somewhat unrealistic. If I had a holodeck, I'd close the door and never come out until I died of exhaustion. It would be hard to convince me I should be anywhere but in the holodeck, getting my oil massage from Cindy Crawford and her simulated twin sister.

Holodecks would be very addicting. If there weren't enough holodecks to go around, I'd get the names of all the people who had reservations ahead of me and beam them into concrete walls. I'd feel tense about it, but that's exactly why I'd need a massage.

I'm afraid the holodeck will be society's last invention.

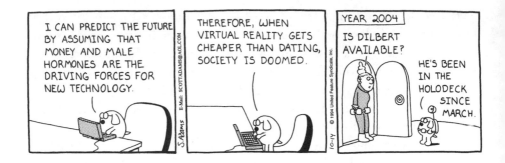

Sex with Aliens

According to *Star Trek,* there are many alien races populated with creatures who would like to have sex with humans. This would open up a lot of anatomical possibilities, but imagine the confusion. It's hard enough to have sex with human beings, much less humanoids. One wrong move and you're suddenly transported naked to the Gamma Quadrant to stand trial for who-knows-what. This could only add to performance anxiety. You would never be quite sure what moves would be sensual and what moves would be a galactic-sized mistake.

Me Trying to Have Sex with an Alien

Me: May I touch that?

Alien: That is not an erogenous zone. It is a separate corporeal being that has been attached to my body for six hundred years.

Me: It's cute. I wonder if it would let me have sex with it.

Alien: That's exactly what I said six hundred years ago.

The best part about having sex with aliens, according to the *Star Trek* model, is that the alien always dies a tragic death soon afterward. I don't have to tell you how many problems that would solve. Realistically, the future won't be that convenient.

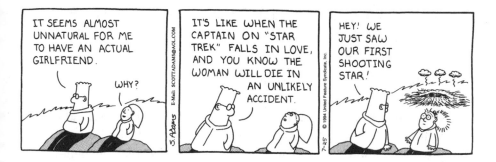

Phasers

I would love to have a device that would stun people into unconsciousness without killing them. I would use it ten times a day. If I got bad service at the convenience store, I'd zap the clerk. If somebody with big hair sat in front of me at the theater, *zap*!

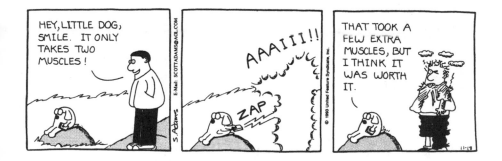

On *Star Trek*, there are no penalties for stunning people with phasers. It happens all the time. All you have to do is claim you were possessed by an alien entity. Apparently, that is viewed as a credible defense in the *Star*

Trek future. Imagine real criminals in a world where the "alien possession" defense is credible.

> **Criminal:** Yes, officer, I did steal that vehicle, and I did kill the occupants, but I was possessed by an evil alien entity.
>
> **Officer:** Well, okay. Move along.

I wish I had a phaser right now. My neighbor's dog likes to stand under my bedroom window on the other side of the fence and bark for hours at a time. My neighbor has employed the bold defense that he believes it might be another neighbor's dog, despite the fact that I am standing there looking at him barking only twenty feet away. In a situation like this, a phaser is really the best approach. I could squeeze off a clean shot through the willow tree. A phaser doesn't make much noise, so it wouldn't disturb anyone. Then the unhappy little dog and I could both get some sleep. If the neighbor complains, I'll explain that the phaser was fired by the other neighbor's dog, a known troublemaker who is said to be invisible.

And if that doesn't work, a photon torpedo is clearly indicated.

Cyborgs

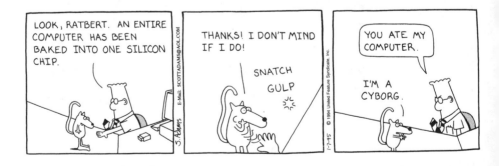

Given the choice, I would rather be a cyborg instead of 100 percent human. I like the thought of technology becoming part of my body. As a human, I am constantly running to the toolbox in my garage to get a tool to deal with some new household malfunction. If I were a cyborg, I might have an electric drill on my arm, plus a metric socket set. That would save a lot of trips. From what I've seen, the cyborg concept is a modular design, so you can add whatever tools you think you'd use most.

I'd love to see crosshairs appear in my viewfinder every time I looked at someone. It would make me feel menacing, and I'd like that. I'd program myself so that anytime I saw a car salesman, a little message would appear in my viewfinder that said "Target Locked On."

It would also be great to have my computer built into my skull. That way I could surf the Net during useless periods of life, such as when people talk to me. All I'd have to do is initiate a head-nodding subroutine during boring conversations and I could amuse myself in my head all day long.

I think that if anyone could become a cyborg, there would be a huge rush of people getting in line for the conversion. Kids would like it for the look. Adults would like it for its utility. Cyborg technology has something for everyone. So, unlike *Star Trek*, I can imagine everyone wanting to be a cyborg.

The only downside I can see is that when the human part dies and you're at the funeral, the cyborg part will try to claw its way out of the casket and slay all the mourners. But that risk can be minimized by saying you have an important business meeting, so you can't make it to the service.

Shields

I wish I had an invisible force field. I'd use it all the time, especially around people who spit when they talk or get too close to my personal space. In fact, I'd probably need a shield quite a bit if I also had a phaser to play with.

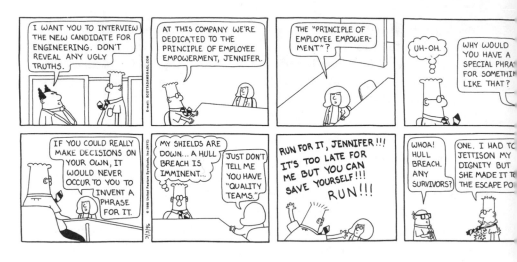

I wouldn't need a big shield system like the one they use to protect the *Enterprise*, maybe just a belt-clip device for personal use. I could insult dangerous people without fear of retribution. Whatever crumbs of personality I now have would be completely unnecessary in the future. On the plus side, it would make shopping much more fun.

Shopping with Shields Up

Me: Ring this up for me, you unpleasant cretin.

Saleswoman: I oughta slug you!

Me: Try it. My shields are up.

Saleswoman: Damn!

Me: There's nothing you can do to harm me.

Saleswoman: I guess you're right. Would you like to open a charge account? Our interest rates are very reasonable.

Me: Nice try.

Tractor Beam

On *Star Trek*, they use tractor beams to retrieve damaged shuttle crafts. I think if that technology were available today, it would be used primarily by boring people to keep their victims within range. I'm glad there are no tractor beams.

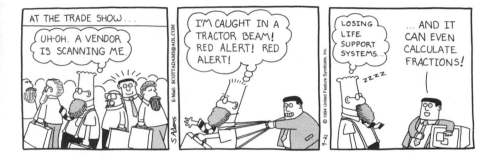

Long-Range Sensors

If people had long-range sensors, they would rarely use them to scan for new signs of life. I think they would use them to avoid work. You could run a continuous scan for your boss and then quickly transport yourself out of the area when he came near. If your manager died in his office, you would know minutes before the authorities discovered him, and that means extra break time.

Vulcan Shoulder Massage

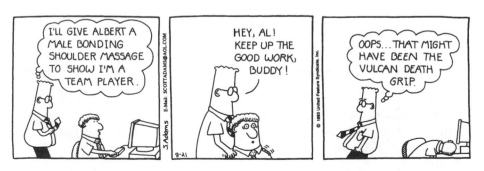

Before all you Trekkies write to correct me, I know there is no such thing as a Vulcan Death Grip even in *Star Trek*. But I wish there were. That would have come in handy many times. It would be easy to make the Vulcan Death Grip look like an accident.

"I was just straightening his collar and he collapsed."

I think the only thing that keeps most people from randomly killing other citizens is the bloody mess it makes and the high likelihood of getting caught. With the Vulcan Death Grip, it would be clean and virtually undetectable. Everybody would be killing people left and right. You wouldn't be able to have a decent conversation at the office over the sound of dead co-workers hitting the carpet. The most common sounds in corporate America would be, "I'm sorry I couldn't give you a bigger raise, but . . . erk!"

And that's why the future won't be like *Star Trek*.

TECHNOLOGY TO AVOID WORK

Much has been written—too much, really—about the technology for making workers more productive. What we really need is technology for helping workers goof off without detection. There's a much bigger market for that. Look at the numbers. For every boss who wants to make you work harder, there are a dozen employees who want to prevent it.

PREDICTION 8

In the future, there will be a huge market for technology products that help workers goof off and still get paid.

Naturally, most of the new goofing off technology will be disguised as productivity tools, just as the current ones are. Employees today goof off with the telephone, e-mail, Internet connections, and their computers. It all looks like work to the unsuspecting employer.

Managers will try to stop employees from any unsanctioned enjoyment at work. They know that enjoyment can lead to high morale and any number of other harmful things. Companies have a variety of technologies for preventing enjoyment. For example, bosses can check logs of phone calls, block access to fun Internet sites, and even snoop on your e-mail. This enjoyment-blocking technology is improving every day.

Companies will give employees ID badges that can be tracked anywhere in the building, so managers can tell how much time you spend reading the newspaper in the restroom, wandering the halls, and hanging out in the cafeteria.

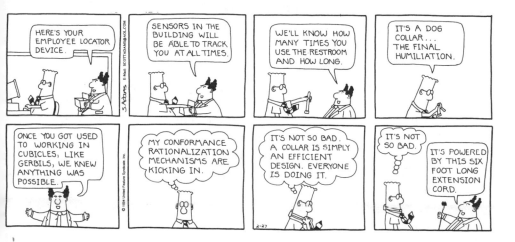

The flaw with the locator-badge concept is that within a month of introduction, an underground market in counterfeit ID badges will spring up. Employees will lock their locator badges in desk drawers and roam freely wearing the fakes. They will not only be free, they will have the added psychological thrill of feeling like they're getting away with something.

It won't be difficult to thwart the locator-badge concept, but employees will need outside help to battle other forms of management-induced evil. That's why you'll see the emergence of a new industry dedicated to helping employees avoid work. I think you'll see advertisements like these in the near future:

Excuse 9000™

The patented Excuse 9000 device will add selected background noise to any phone conversation, giving you the perfect alibi for not being at work. Need a flat tire alibi? No problem. Just set the Excuse 9000 for "Highway Noise" and leave your boss a voice-mail message from the comfort of your own bed. Other noises in the basic starter pack include: airliner going down, deep-lung coughing, and armed intruder.

WorkSurfer™

Is your evil employer monitoring which web sites you visit during the day? Is it getting harder to satisfy your daily requirement of online comics, sports news, and pornography while pretending to work? We've got the answer in the WorkSurfer. We'll e-mail you the web pages you specify every day from a new, untraceable address. WorkSurfer costs only $20 per month, and our invoice lists the service as "Three Ring Binders," so you can hide it on a voucher and make your boss pay!

BuzzCut™

This advanced software will strip the buzzwords out of any e-mail you receive from your boss and give you what you need to know.

Example:

Boss's e-mail: We must facilitate the redesign of our core processes to optimize customer satisfaction.

BuzzCut Translation: Hey, I wrote a memo!

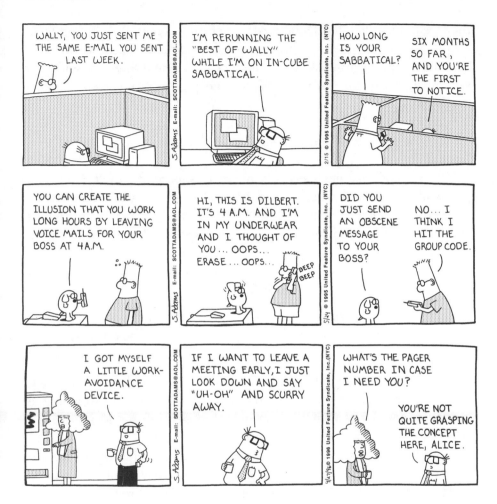

THE FUTURE OF THE INTERNET

Experts predict the Internet will slow down or blow up because of increasing traffic. They're all wrong. I know this because I'm a guy.

I remember the joy when my cartoon syndicate, United Media, told me they were upgrading the Dilbert Zone web site from a T1 link to a DS3. (DS3 is a very fast speed—a "big pipe" as they say in the business.)

When I told other people about the new DS3 pipe, I found myself sniffing smugly, yanking up my pants, taking a deep breath, and actually talking in a hillbilly drawl:

"Yup, we got us a DS3 now. Whatcha runnin' on yers?"

When I described my telecommunications superiority, I felt manly and powerful. Colors seemed more vivid. I felt alive, albeit alive as a hillbilly.

There are millions of people like me—males who care a great deal about the speed of the Internet. They want speed. They need it. They'll find a way to get it.

PREDICTION 9

In the future, Internet capacity will increase indefinitely to keep up with the egos of the people using it. Cost will not be an issue.

Obviously, there are millions of women using and building the Internet, too, but on average they don't care the same way men do. For women, the Internet is a tool. For men, it's personal. Men are obsessed about the size of their pipes, whereas women claim it "doesn't matter."

It won't be economical for companies to keep buying equipment to meet the growing Internet demand. At first glance, that would seem to be a big problem, but that economic gap can be filled through a common business process called "lying like a filthy weasel."

As I write this, technical professionals around the world are writing proposals for Internet funding and trying not to laugh so hard that they get spittle on the final hard copy. These proposals will make their way to high-ranking executives (mostly males) who will skim the document, become thoroughly boggled, and come away with just one message:

Your pipe is very small.

The frightened male executives will immediately approve funding for bigger pipes. Then they will sniff smugly, yank up their pants, take deep breaths, and begin talking with hillbilly drawls. It won't be pretty.

All of the technical professionals who created these lies will switch jobs with other professionals in their industry and begin implementing their predecessors' plans. Later, they'll all blame "the last guy" for lying about the true costs. This is how the Internet will be funded indefinitely.

CLOTHING OF THE FUTURE

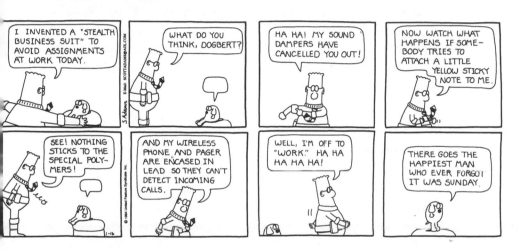

My clothes don't do enough for me. All they do is cover my naughty parts and keep me warm. And they don't even do that right, because in the summer I'm too warm. My clothes are Induhviduals. I want smarter clothes.

PREDICTION 10

In the future, your clothes will be smarter than you.

I have great expectations for clothes of the future. I want my clothes to keep me at the perfect temperature all day. I want my clothes to tickle me when I'm sad. My clothes should sense danger and electrically stimulate my leg muscles so I run away before I even know what the problem is.

I want transmitters in my clothes to tell my house what room I'm in at all times. I will walk from room to room like Moses parting the Red Sea, the lighting and temperature adjusting to suit my personal preferences. The people who are already in those rooms won't like it one bit, but I'm sure Moses had his critics, too. You can't let the opinions of other people get to you.

I want my clothes to have a fake Batman-like muscular torso and head cover. That way I'll look more like a studly superhero and less like a little bald guy.

And I want a cellular phone built into the head cover so I have yet another way to insult gullible Induhviduals to their faces without fear of retribution.

Me: You're the most gullible imbecile I've ever met.

Induhvidual: What did you call me?

Me: Shhh! I'm on the phone.

Induhvidual: Oh, sorry.

I want my clothes to have stealth technology so I can avoid all the people who ask for my help. I want stealth technology that is so good, I can walk into a car dealer's lot carrying a tub full of cash and not draw any attention. I want to absorb radar so I can speed without getting caught. I want to leer at attractive women without detection. I want to sneeze on the buffet and blame the guy behind me.

I want clothes that have a nonstick surface so food stains slide off. I want clothes that can be cleaned by taking them outside and shaking them vigorously. (You'll be naked when you go outside because you'll only have one of these expensive garments. But it won't matter that much because the neighbors will think the person who lives in your house has much better torso muscles, so you must be a visitor.)

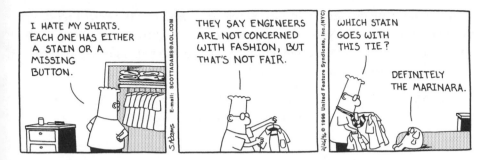

The clothes of the future will create some new risks. They'll be so valuable that muggers will steal your clothes and leave your wallet. Crooks will be frolicking around town in your jumpsuit making long distance calls with the built-in phone while you're hiding naked in an alley. And you won't be able to find help, because the other pedestrians will have the stealth feature of their own clothes turned on so people like you can't locate them.

It won't necessarily be a good thing to be the first person in your town to have the clothes of the future. For example, if someone wants to use your phone, you'll have to say no, because your only phone will be built into your clothes. If they insist, you'll have to let them wear your jumpsuit. When you try to get your clothes back, they'll turn on the stealth feature and disappear for days. Your friends will be taking joyrides in your jumpsuit while you're sitting around the house naked. That's why I don't make friends.

THE NETWORK COMPUTER VERSUS THE PERSONAL COMPUTER

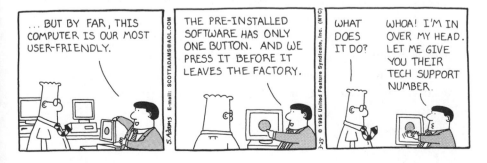

Many technology forecasters are wondering whether the new breed of Network Computers (NCs) will replace Personal Computers (PCs). On the off chance that you are not familiar with the NC versus PC debate, allow me to provide some background:

> The NC is blah, blah, blah, Java, blah, blah, trying to screw Microsoft, blah, blah, no hard disk, blah, blah, Larry Ellison.

Those are the pertinent points. I'd give more details, but frankly, if you haven't heard of Network Computers already, you'll probably just skim this section looking for naughty words.

If you don't understand all of the technical issues, don't worry that you are an ignoramus. I will compensate by typing this section slowly. And you really don't need to know the technical differences between NCs and PCs in order to drink fully of the beauty and elegance of my arguments that follow.

You do need to know that an NC is essentially a PC with no hard drive (or a tiny one). An NC downloads software from the Internet and executes it on an as-needed basis. The main advantage of the NC is that it will be cheaper and easier to use than a PC—but it will do less.

The driving force behind the NC is the belief that the companies who brought us things like Unix, relational databases, and Windows can make an appliance that is inexpensive and easy to use if they choose to do that. This is a bit like hiring Doctor Kevorkian to be the physician at your day care center, but I'm getting ahead of my point here.

There have been many spirited and stimulating debates about the relative technical merits of the NC versus the PC. This debate is an important one primarily because technology magazines can't sell advertisements if the rest of the magazine is empty. The NC has filled that important void.

A brilliant futurist such as myself doesn't need to wallow around in the technical differences between the NC and the PC in order to make spookily accurate predictions. Let us instead find relevant parallels in history on which to base our prediction.

First, look at the arguments put forth by the proponents of the NC.

PRO-NC ARGUMENT	**COUNTERARGUMENT**
Many people will prefer a low-cost solution, even if it means giving up some functionality and prestige.	One word: Yugo.
The NC will be much easier to use than full-blown PCs, thus guaranteeing a dominant market share.	One word: Macintosh.
This new computing paradigm will neuter Microsoft's stranglehold on the PC industry.	One word: Bill.

Some people will argue that Bill Gates and Microsoft aren't smart enough to stop NC's threat to the PC market. But don't forget, Bill Gates is the guy who turned Apple Computer into a no-cost Microsoft R&D center and made everyone believe it was a separate company, thus reducing antitrust complaints. Then he launched Windows 95 to make it seem like he couldn't possibly be that smart.

How smart is he really? Smart enough not to let you know how smart he is. Or to put it another way, if he ever decides to slay a family member, I don't think you'll find his bloody glove at the scene.

Now let's say, for argument, that the NC started to become a big threat to Microsoft. Would Bill Gates watch the value of his $20 billion in Microsoft stock shrink to zero, or would he make one of the following strategic moves:

Potential Strategic Moves

1. Bundle a free NC with every copy of Windows 95.

2. Create strategic alliances with the NC companies and act "helpful."

I think you can see that either of these choices would work. So Microsoft should come out of this okay.

No matter what happens in the overall market, there will certainly be plenty of demand for NCs in places like prisons, libraries, and airports, but the home market will be hard to crack. The companies who make NCs will have to do some sophisticated market segmentation analysis. Or they can just read the sophisticated analysis that I include here for your convenience:

CUSTOMER PROFILE	LIKELY TO BUY
This person always wants the latest computer, no matter how complicated or expensive.	Personal Computer (PC) based on Intel chip and Windows software.
Same as above, but supports public television. Dreams of quitting job and becoming an artist. Might have a goatee.	Macintosh computer.
Same as first profile, but enjoys pain and has no friends. Might be portly and wear suspenders.	Unix workstation.
This person thinks that a computer would look lovely with the furniture and wants to "check out that Internet" someday to do some shopping and maybe book airline tickets. Might work in senior management.	Network Computer (NC).

This NC-buying group won't be able to handle too much complexity in a computer. The NC manufacturers know that, of course, but I predict they will still vastly overestimate the intelligence of the target market.

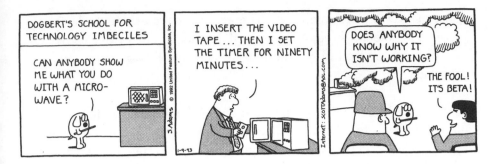

To illustrate my point, I heard this story about a computer technician who services corporate PCs: .

True Story

When the technician enters the office of especially clueless-looking managers, he gives them this computing advice: "Once in a while, you have to stretch the computer cables out straight. That's because the data is digital, which means it's all ones and zeroes. The zeroes can make it through the bent cable okay, because they have smooth edges, but the ones can get stuck."

I'll bet there are still managers throughout this technician's territory who straighten their cables on a regular basis. I'm guessing some even put binders beneath their PCs so the data will run downhill.

Do you need more convincing? A *Dilbert* reader recently told me this story.

True Story

The copy machine was near a thermostat control box on the wall. An office prankster put a sign over the thermostat box with instructions to speak into the microphone to control the copier with voice commands. There was much merriment when one member of the staff inserted his document in the copy machine, walked to the thermostat, and said, "Two copies, no staple."

Most new NC customers will take it out of the box and try to randomly plug the cables into whatever orifices they can find around the house, hoping to get lucky. If you see your neighbor's dog growling and scooting its tail on the ground, you can be sure its owner just got an NC.

Then there's the complex issue of whether the power needs to be turned on in order for the NC to function properly. That might seem silly to you Brainiacs who are smart enough to read *Dilbert* books, but believe me, many people are routinely stumped by this question.

If you call the tech support number for your computer and tell them that your printer is not working, the first question they will ask is, "Is it turned on?" If you pass that portion of the intelligence test they will ask, "Is it connected to your computer?"

They don't ask these questions simply to belittle you and insult your intelligence, although it's obvious they enjoy that aspect of the transaction, too. No, they ask because experience shows they can solve many problems with those two questions. You can never underestimate the stupidity of the general public.

I contend that the term "easy-to-use computer" is an oxymoron. The NC will be the physical proof. It will provide the final answer to the question, "Just how dumb are people, anyway?"

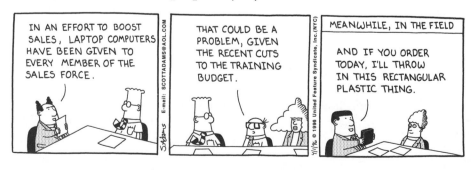

Despite the fact that the typical NC customer will be thoroughly unable to operate the device, I predict a healthy market demand. This prediction is based on an in-depth analysis of the kinds of products most similar to the NC: home exercise equipment.

I recently bought one of those trendy new exercise devices—the kind that builds muscles that are useful only for mowing your lawn and pulling on tight panty hose, neither of which I do. (I pay a guy to come over once a week to pull my tight panty hose on for me.)

When I first saw a picture of that fiendish-looking exercise device, I thought that it would be boring, painful, and annoying to use. But I was greatly influenced by the television commercial, which featured attractive women who do unrelated kinds of exercises in order to look the way they do. When I saw the ad, I said, "That's good enough for me!" and I dialed the 800 number immediately. After all, if you can't believe paid models, who can you believe? The exercise machine is in my garage under some boxes.

People will buy NCs for the same reason they buy exercise machines: an irrational need. People who buy exercise machines believe it will make them healthy and thin. People who will buy NCs will believe they will make them technically sophisticated and knowledgeable about the Web.

When I worked at Pacific Bell, one of my jobs was giving demonstrations of our fast digital telephone lines (ISDN, actually) to helpless, trapped customers who didn't know why they were there. We would lure them into the lab to watch stimulating technical displays such as "file transfers" and "digital telephony."

The customers' eyes would glaze over. Although we were showing them useful and valuable services, the demonstrations acted like verbal lobotomies. The poor, pathetic customers would sit there as though shot by boredom-filled darts. If we wanted to, I'm sure we could have put them into cages, loaded them into Range Rovers, and transported them to a remote forest for release. (We only did that once, and we caught hell for it.)

Toward the end of the demonstration, just before the customers' souls could abandon their cold, lifeless shells, I would fire up a demonstration of a new thing (it was new then) called the World Wide Web. The only thing you could do with the Web at the time was call up twelve dinosaur pictures and maybe look at some precious gems from the Smithsonian collection, unless their server wasn't working, which it usually wasn't. The Web was slow, unreliable, and totally void of useful information, but the customers' eyes would widen when they saw it. They would stand up and demand permission to use the mouse and click on this "Internet thing" themselves. Then they would start grilling me about what they needed to buy. They wanted to be able to look at dinosaurs and gems themselves. And they wanted it bad.

I witnessed pure technology lust. The customers were literally having a physical response to the Web. It was like a drug to them. And it happened to every type of customer we brought to the lab. It defied explanation. People became instantly irrational. They became immune to issues of value, cost, and complexity. All they knew is that they wanted it.

This experience convinced me that any analysis of the NC's merits is a waste of time. People will buy them. They will buy lots of them. Many will choose it over the PC simply because it costs less. They won't care that it has less functionality, because they are immune to the question of its value.

PREDICTION 11

In the future, Network Computers will be purchased and used with the same enthusiasm as home exercise equipment.

Or, as I like to say, "If you build it, they will be dumb."

ISDN

There are two things that any company needs in order to bring a bold new technology to market:

1. Stupidity.

2. See 1.

Whenever bold new technologies are created, the poor bastards who create them find out the market isn't ready or the technology isn't refined enough. The innovator rarely makes money. Then some clever company comes in and sees what went wrong, corrects the bone-headed mistakes, and makes it all work. In general, it is always better to be a clever company than a poor bastard.

So why would any company ever introduce a new technology knowing that the odds are stacked against them? They do it because they have just the right mix of stupidity and stock options. Thank goodness for that. Otherwise, civilization would never advance. We'd be sitting around in leaf beds picking bugs out of each other's fur. And frankly, I don't want to touch your fur.

Speaking of bugs in fur, let's talk about ISDN, a subject I know from my days as an employee at Pacific Bell. If you're not familiar with ISDN, the letters represent four words that don't mean anything useful when you string them all together. This is a perfect metaphor for ISDN, and, in retrospect, I'm certain it's what the developers intended.

The basic idea with ISDN is that your local phone company can convert your existing telephone wires into a nifty high-speed digital path from you to anyplace else. You can use ISDN lines for everything from phone calls to video conferencing. Most people use ISDN to connect to the Internet at speeds up to 128 kilobytes per second. This improves productivity, because it allows you to view online *Dilbert* cartoons without cutting into your work time. The phone companies don't spell that out in the brochures, but I think we all know what they mean.

According to the telephone companies, ISDN is very "flexible," meaning it can do many things. According to the customers, ISDN is a "frustrating piece of crap," because it can do many things, thereby making it nearly impossible to figure out how to make it do any one particular thing.

Calling ISDN "flexible" is like saying a drowning victim has moist skin. It's technically true, but you're not impressed. There is such a thing as too much of a good thing. That's the problem with ISDN.

I worked in Pacific Bell's ISDN lab for a few years and got to see many people try to make an ISDN connection work. I have yet to see anybody succeed on the first try, even by luck.

The odds are impossibly stacked against the unwitting ISDN customer. ISDN equipment can have a thousand possible options with unfathomable names like "SPID" and "TEI." Even if you figure out what the acronyms mean, no amount of common sense can help you sort out what goes where. (Many new Induhviduals were procreated during ISDN testing. Refer to Chapter 1.)

With some technology, you get the feeling that the designers weren't fully considering its ease of use. With ISDN, you get the feeling that the designers hate your friggin' guts. I'm not saying they *do* actually hate you, but I never saw anything to disprove the theory.

If somehow you set all the options correctly on the ISDN equipment on your desk, you still have to deal with the options on the ISDN line itself. Those are set by the phone company per your instructions. There are a thousand possible settings, depending on how you plan to use it and what kind of equipment the phone company uses for your neighborhood. That adds another thousand things to go wrong. Then you have to select a long-distance phone service for your ISDN connection. That adds a few more options that can be set wrong.

When you order an ISDN line, the phone company will ask how you want the options set on the line. But how do you know? The company that sold you your ISDN equipment won't tell you what you need. If the information is in their documentation, it's spread across multiple chapters. You have a better chance of finding Jimmy Hoffa in your documentation than you have of finding the information you need to order an ISDN line.

All I've talked about so far is the confusion on one end of the ISDN connection. There has to be something on the other end of the connection or it's somewhat pointless. The other end generally has a different set of equipment and often a different flavor of ISDN service from the phone company. That's another several thousand potential problems.

I'm exaggerating a bit, but let's say your odds of getting ISDN to work on the first try are a billion to one against you. This is higher than the real number, but not by a meaningful margin. The question is, Why would the phone companies think they could sell something like that?

It's my fault.

Prior to working in Pacific Bell's ISDN lab, I worked on ISDN strategy. It was my job to recommend whether the company should go hog-wild and make ISDN available all over California or just slink away from it in shame. Here's my story.

The way I see it, there are three possible paths for every major corporate recommendation:

1. The right way.

2. The wrong way.

3. The weasel way.

The right way would require too much honesty for you to keep your job. The wrong way would require lying, and that would be bad, especially if you got caught. The path I chose—the weasel way—allows you to be completely honest, but in a way that puts the blame on someone else when everything goes to hell.

I studied the market for ISDN and calculated all of its costs. I found that it was a great technology with no immediate competition, and it probably had a large market potential. The only thing that could limit its success was complete incompetence on the part of all the phone companies, colossal stupidity by every single ISDN hardware vendor, and complete idiocy on the part of the regulatory oversight bodies.

It was obvious to me that ISDN was doomed.

Since ISDN had been around for years already without making money, it attracted more than its share of slugs, malcontents, and blithering Induhviduals who couldn't get meaningful work elsewhere. There was a smattering of bright, well-meaning people working with ISDN, but they were outnumbered and rendered totally harmless.

This situation made it difficult to present my findings in an objective fashion. I couldn't stand in front of the senior executives of Pacific Bell and say, "All of the problems with ISDN are caused by the most amazing collection of morons that history has ever known. I expect the bad news to continue unabated. Let's run like frightened rabbits."

Instead, when it came time to make my presentation, I carefully described the economic opportunity that could spring from a hypothetical future of well-designed ISDN equipment and superlative operational support. I pointed out that all of the current problems were human-created and human-solvable. All it would take was the intelligence and professionalism of employees and vendors working as a team. I recommended full steam ahead.

The executives asked some probing questions to test my analysis, questions like, "Why is the expense line bumpy?" I bobbed and weaved and made it out of the meeting without ever telling a lie.

ISDN was studied many more times by employees and consultants who had the same dilemma that I had. I assume they took the weasel way too, since Pacific Bell has been deploying ISDN like crazy. No doubt the other phone companies noticed the enthusiasm that Pacific Bell displayed for ISDN and assigned their own people to study it more thoroughly, creating the same weasel way results.

The big question everyone asks about ISDN is whether it has a future. Will the average person use it for fast connections to the Internet or will they use some future service through their cable television company? I can answer that question with the same analytical skill that brought you ISDN in the first place. But first, some background.

Cable companies have what appears to be a huge technical advantage— a big coaxial cable into your house that can carry far more information than a phone line with ISDN service. Most pundits argue that this advantage will be enough for the cable companies to trounce ISDN in the market of the future. This argument misses one important fact:

> Cable companies are staffed with people who couldn't get jobs at telephone companies.

No matter how many technical advantages the cable companies start with, it's a huge hairy deal to change their networks for two-way communications. The technology exists, but making it work will require the intelligence and professionalism of thousands of cable company employees and vendors working as a team. Obviously, cable companies are doomed.

When cable companies add the departments needed to support a two-way transmission service, they will become tangled and bloated. Their resources will be devoured by "technical standards meetings," "quality initiatives," and continuous pointless reorganizations.

Every time their technical people build a test network, the marketing requirements will change. Every time they test a new set-top box for the home, a newer and better one will become available. Meanwhile, cable company employees are giving weasel way presentations to their own management and recommending full steam ahead.

Telephone companies had a running start with ISDN—they already knew how to provide two-way phone services—and it has still taken them ten years to improve from total incompetence with ISDN to mild incompetence. Meanwhile, the cable companies are painting targets on their shoes, cleaning their guns, and laughing like tickled hermits over the fact that their cables are thicker. Poor bastards.

I predict the cable companies will flounder for at least ten years in their attempts to offer two-way data service to the home. You'll see hundreds of trials and dozens of small-scale overhyped services, but nothing substantial. By then, ISDN will be simpler to use and widely available.

ISDN works great after you figure out how to set the options. The only thing that stands between ISDN and market success is ease of use, and that has improved each year. In effect, the phone companies will be both the poor bastards who developed ISDN—and failed—and the clever companies who figured out what went wrong and fixed it.

Technology is impossible to predict, but stupidity is a known constant. ISDN service has experienced the highest saturation of stupidity of any service you can think of. And it survived. That's what I call robust. That makes ISDN a good bet.

The cable companies are still at the beginning of their stupidity saturation phase. They have to pass through the poor bastard failure before they can become a threat to ISDN. In the near term, the best we can hope for is that we won't lose our television reception completely.

PREDICTION 12

In the future, ISDN services will improve to the point where you can mention it in a crowd without generating laughter.

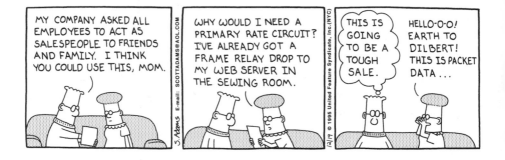

THE BOZO FILTER

One of my biggest problems in life is the constant stream of complaints, dumb questions, and inane opinions that other people burden me with. I don't want new ways to communicate, I want new ways to stop the people who are trying to communicate with me. I know I'm not alone, even though I wish I were.

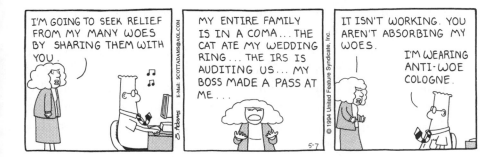

Every day, I get e-mail from someone who says something like, "How do you get ideas? Please tell me how you do it so I can get ideas, too."

I do not know how to answer that inquiry without insulting the person. I don't want to say, "I'm sorry to report that if your brain does not create any ideas, you are dead. This is hell."

And I can't say, "Everyone gets ideas. If you're getting bad ones, it must be because your brain is defective."

And I can't say, "I'm far to busy to be bothered with your insignificant and ludicrous question. Thank you for writing. Please pick up the latest *Dilbert* book."

And I can't say the truth—that I look at Garfield and change the cat jokes to fit Dogbert, add a few corporate buzzwords, and pass it off as original.

There's really no graceful way out. So I find myself wishing I had never gotten the question in the first place. I wish I had—to borrow a phrase from Guy Kawasaki at Apple Computers—a "Bozo Filter." I mean no disrespect to Bozo the Clown when I say this. I would enjoy getting a message from the real Bozo. You expect a famous clown to be able to send funny e-mail messages, unless he just doesn't care anymore.

The Bozo Filter would be software that checks incoming e-mail and weeds out the ones that are worthless. The worthless ones always have tell-tale signs. The filter would easily find them.

For example, when I get an e-mail message that has fifty other addressees and the phrase "I thought you might be interested in this," I want my software to delete that message immediately. And I want the originator of that message to be added to my list of people who are forever banned from my electronic kingdom.

About three times a day, different people forward the same e-mail messages to me about an alleged incident involving Neiman-Marcus and their secret cookie recipe. This is a famous urban legend. The gist of it is that someone supposedly asked for cookies at Neiman-Marcus and then, through a misunderstanding, was charged a bundle for their secret cookie recipe instead. The alleged angry customer is now getting revenge by spreading the alleged secret recipe all over the net. I want my Bozo Filter to look for the words "Neiman-Marcus" and "cookies" and reject those messages. And I want a mild electric shock sent back through the Internet to whoever thought I needed to see that.

Once or twice a day, I get an e-mail message with the phrase "cup holder" in it. This is another urban legend that several hundred people have told me has happened to them or a friend. This story involves a computer user who calls technical support to report a broken cup holder on the computer. The cup holder turns out to be the CD-ROM drive tray. I want my Bozo Filter to prevent me from ever seeing this message again. And I want the lying weasels who say they took that tech support phone call to be locked in a room and forced to fight it out until there is really only one left. This might be more than the software can deliver, but I can dream.

PREDICTION 13

In the future, we'll all use sophisticated Bozo Filters to prevent idiots from communicating with us.

The Bozo Filter will definitely be available for e-mail. America Online already lets you block certain e-mail addresses. And if you use Claris Emailer software, for example, you can search for keywords in incoming software and have them prioritized or filed automatically. I want the filters to extend to the telephone system, too.

I want my voice-mail system to compensate for the Induhviduals who leave messages. In particular, I want these features:

Auctioneer Mode: Speeds up messages left by people who speak too slowly.

First Ten/Last Ten: Deletes everything except the first and last ten seconds of a message. The stuff in the middle is never worth listening to anyway.

Rambler's Nudge: A rude voice that interrupts callers who are leaving overly long messages and says, "Just leave your stinkin' phone number, will ya? I HAVE A LIFE!"

Number Watcher: Voice recognition system that listens to see if the caller mumbles an unintelligible return phone number. If so, a voice will break in and say, "What language is that—Mumblican? Spit out your sandwich and try it again."

My telephone system should also have a voice-stress analyzer to filter out Induhviduals before the phone even rings.

Bozo Filter:	This is Scott Adams's Bozo Filter. Please answer yes or no. Will this phone call benefit Scott Adams in any way?
Caller:	Um . . . yes. Yes, it will.
Bozo Filter:	Liar! *Click.*

If I can't shut out all the Induhviduals in my life, I think I should be compensated for listening to them. That's only fair. When our Bozo Filters become good enough to prevent Induhviduals from getting freebies, they will certainly be willing to pay us to listen.

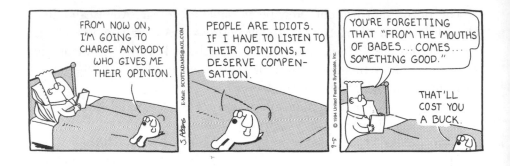

CENSORSHIP ON THE INTERNET

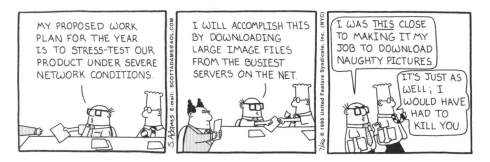

When I meet people, I can tell immediately whether they were harmed by exposure to dirty pictures when they were kids. The people who viewed dirty pictures tend to be cynical and sarcastic. More often than not they are syndicated cartoonists. But those who were lucky enough to be sheltered from the effects of obscene pictures are monks now. I'm overgeneralizing, of course. There's lots of gray area. For example, some people looked at pictures of themselves naked and they become gay monks, but these are the exceptions and not the rule.

In the future, greater efforts will be made to protect young people from pornography on the information superhighway. I'm totally in favor of that. Those kids should get their pornography the same way the kids of my generation did—by shoplifting. Granted, my generation suffered some ill effects from exposure to pornography, but at least we were learning a trade in the process of getting it. Kids today don't have to leave the house. They can fire up the computer and fill their hard drives with free pornography. At least that's what I've been told.

While researching this chapter, I tried to find obscene pictures on the Internet that didn't require a credit card to view. I fired up an Internet "search engine" and input several words that are too disgusting to mention. I hoped it would tell me where to find all the pornography.

And did it ever. Whoo hoo! I tried one location after another and found that the servers were all too overloaded with traffic to be viewable. I concluded from this experience that the Internet is already safe for children.

Kids have shorter attention spans than adults. They would never sit in front of a blank screen for hours on the slight chance that they might see something naughty at some undetermined time in the future. It's not a competitive use of time. In terms of arousal per second, there's a much better payoff from flipping through your mom's Victoria's Secret catalogs. Remember, we're talking about kids here—mostly boys—and if they're anything like I was, all it takes is a commercial for *Wheel of Fortune* and you're off to the races. Hello Vanna! The Internet is overkill when you're thirteen years old.

By my estimate, you'd have to be at least twenty-one years old before you'd be willing to sit in front of a blank screen for several minutes waiting for pictures of naked people. There's a natural protection built into the Internet, because people get more patient with age; and the nastier the pictures on the Internet, the longer you have to wait to see them. Logically then, all sexually explicit Internet sites will be jammed with traffic from horny adults (and authors doing research), because these people have the most patience.

PREDICTION 14

In the future, kids won't have access to online pornography, because the X-rated Internet sites will be clogged by horny adults who have more patience.

Companies will still be able to make a fortune selling products that block minors from pornography, but technical solutions can only go so far. In my opinion, we don't need more technology to block sexually oriented Internet sites; we need more horny old people to jam them with traffic. This is a very good use for horny old people. Frankly, it's the only one I can think of. And since these horny old people are usually parents, you get the added bonus of parental involvement.

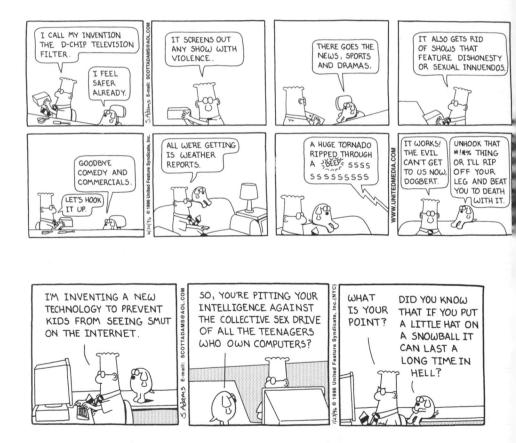

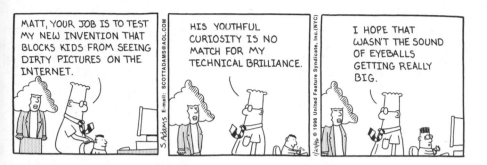

TECHNOLOGY MAKES US LESS PRODUCTIVE

I love computers. To me, computers are like tangerines, in the sense that I can't make a good analogy about either one of them right now. But if I could, it would involve a clever point about how computers are fun even though they create a lot of work. Here are some of my favorite cartoons on that point.

PREDICTION 15

In the future, technology will continue to make our lives harder and many of us will be delighted about it

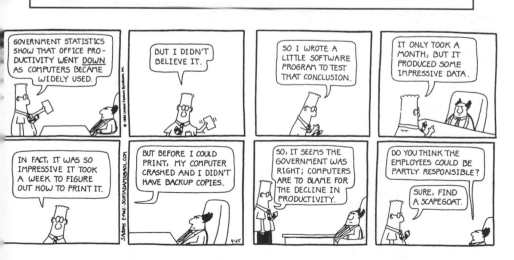

THANK YOU ALL FOR COMING TO OUR ENGINEERING QUALITY TEAM MEETING.
TODAY WE'LL TRY TO IDENTIFY THE ROOT CAUSE OF OUR SLOW DESIGN PROCESS.
LET ME TAKE SOME WILD GUESSES HERE.
MANAGEMENT KEEPS INCREASING OUR WORK AND CUTTING OUR STAFF.
WE SPEND ALL OUR TIME GIVING STATUS REPORTS TO UNNECESSARY LAYERS OF MANAGEMENT!!
NOW WE'RE HAVING ALL-DAY MEETINGS TO TALK ABOUT OUR INEFFICIENCY!!
I WAS KINDA HOPING FOR SOMETHING THAT ISN'T ANYBODY'S FAULT.
OUR COMPUTERS ARE TOO SLOW. WE NEED NEW ONES.
NOW WE'RE GETTING SOMEPLACE.
S. Adams E-Mail: SCOTTADAMS@AOL.COM
© 1994 United Feature Syndicate, Inc.
5-1

EXPAND... WINDOW
WELL, LOOK WHO GOT A VOICE-CONTROLLED COMPUTER.
INSERT... COLUMN
IF I WERE A LESSER ENGINEER I MIGHT BE ENVIOUS.
ADD... ROW
I DON'T MIND USING MY PREHISTORIC MOUSE-DRIVEN COMPUTER.
AND I'M NOT BITTER ABOUT MY REQUEST FOR A COLOR PRINTER BEING DENIED!
AT LEAST I WON'T WORK ALL DAY THEN ACCIDENTALLY...
DELETE... A FILE!!
PLEASE... NOT IN FRONT OF THE COMPUTER.
S. Adams E-Mail: SCOTTADAMS@AOL.COM
© 1994 United Feature Syndicate, Inc.
4-24

LET'S GO AROUND THE TABLE AND SHARE OUR ACCOMPLISHMENTS.
I CREATED A DOCUMENT THIS WEEK.
BUT THIS IS NO ORDINARY DOCUMENT!
I BOUGHT A $500 DESKTOP PUBLISHING PROGRAM AND TOOK A TWO-DAY CLASS TO LEARN IT.
I INCORPORATED DIGITIZED PHOTOS AND COLOR HIGHLIGHTS IN A MULTI-COLUMN PAGE LAYOUT!
CLIP-ART ICONS ARE SPRINKLED LIBERALLY AROUND THE PAGE TO FORM A VISUAL MOSAIC!
NEXT WEEK – GOD WILLING – I'LL ADD A TOPIC AND SOME CONTENT.
DO YOU REMEMBER WHEN I SAID YOU SHOULD ENJOY YOUR WORK?
I DIDN'T MEAN IT.
OOH

I JUST GOT OUR CONSULTANT'S REPORT. HE'S IDENTIFIED OUR BIGGEST PROBLEM.
E-mail: SCOTTADAMS@AOL.COM
I RECOMMEND THAT WE BUILD A TRACKING DATABASE.
WE CAN PUT IT ON THE NETWORK.
© 1996 United Feature Syndicate, Inc.(NYC)
WOULD YOU LIKE TO HEAR WHAT THE PROBLEM IS FIRST?
I HATE TO DWELL ON THE NEGATIVE.
WE LIKE DATABASES.

YOU HAVEN'T HEARD WHAT THE PROBLEM IS YET; HOW CAN YOU RECOMMEND BUILDING A DATABASE TO SOLVE IT??
E-mail: SCOTTADAMS@AOL.COM
WE ALWAYS BUILD A DATABASE.
AND WE'LL NEED COFFEE MUGS FOR THE PROJECT TEAM.
© 1996 United Feature Syndicate, Inc.(NYC)
THE PROBLEM IS THAT WE HAVE POOR PROCESSES.
THAT COULD BE THE SLOGAN ON OUR MUGS!

ENERGY SOURCES

Scientists will eventually stop flailing around with solar power and focus their efforts on harnessing the only truly unlimited source of energy on the planet: stupidity.

PREDICTION 16

In the future, scientists will learn how to convert
stupidity into clean fuel.

The challenge will be in figuring out how to control this bountiful resource. I predict that the energy companies will place huge hamster wheels outside of convenience stores and offer free lottery tickets to people who spend five minutes running in them. The hamster wheels will be connected to power generators. This plan will produce an unlimited supply of cheap power.

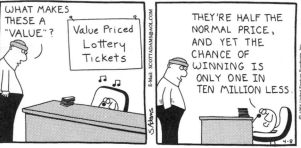
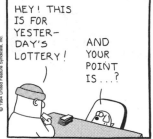

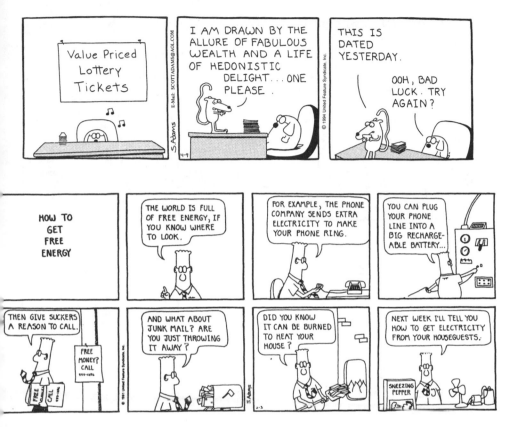

I predict that wind power will finally become a viable large-scale energy source, but not because of better windmill technology. We will discover more wind—the flapping of people's mouths.

All that's needed to harness this wind is a critical mass of people and a controversial topic. I predict you'll see windmills near Macintosh-user group meetings. A representative from the power utility company will be planted in the audience. At a strategic time during each meeting, he will stand up and say, "The Windows platform seems just as good as the Macintosh. Why don't we all just switch?"

An accomplice will quickly open the door facing the row of windmills and get out of the way.

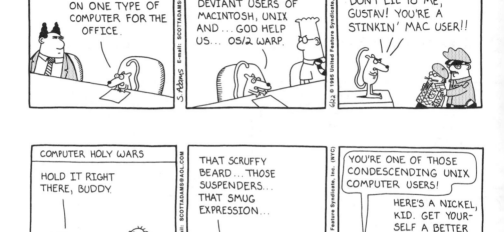

TECHNOLOGY AS THE LEADING CAUSE OF DEATH

At the moment, the leading cause of death is heart disease. That will change in the future, not because we'll cure heart disease, but because we'll come up with many more ways to accidentally kill healthy people.

PREDICTION 17

In the future, technology will become the leading cause of death.

If you think about it, human beings are the worst possible creatures to have access to powerful technology. It would be much better for everyone if, for example, fish were the ones with all the technology. They wouldn't be able to push the buttons with their little fins. No humans would get hurt, and the fish would be able to brag about their great stuff until eventually it all turned into protective barrier reefs.

But it's not a perfect world, and fish don't own all the technology. Humans do. That's bad, because technology magnifies the ability of one person to have a big impact on other people. If that doesn't scare you, then the next time you see professional wrestling on television, look at the crowd shots and ask yourself if you'd like those people to have a bigger impact on your life.

There's no required safety testing for technology. I think that's because the danger doesn't seem obvious to the casual observer. That's what futurists like myself are for—to scare the bejeezus out of you for no useful purpose whatsoever.

Let's get on with that important work.

Television is our biggest threat as a species, but not because of the sex and violence. It's because Hollywood pipes an endless stream of impossibly attractive people into our consciousness.

It's awfully hard to get naked in front of someone who has just watched *Body Shaping* on ESPN ... especially if your partner points the remote control at you and starts clicking it desperately. Nobody needs that.

If television doesn't ruin our ability to mate, the conversations about technology will. For the first time in history, it's possible to have a conversation with someone who speaks the same language and yet have no idea what the topic is. The problem is mostly with men. Women are better conversationalists, and they tend to contain their talk about technology. Men have less verbal awareness. We'll keep yammering about things like subsecond response times, CPU cycles, and bandwidth until there's bloodshed.

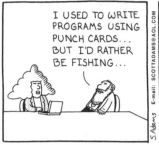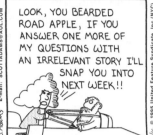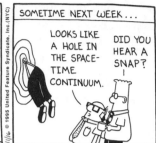

Technology allows us to put more of our lives in the hands of engineers every day. This might not scare those of you who work in nonengineering companies, but personally, it's enough to make me wake up screaming every night. I know a lot of engineers.

We all know that big companies make economic decisions about the trade-offs between price and safety. That's understandable. It only gets scary when you realize that engineers are the ones who are making those calculations. And engineers don't like people. In my nightmares, just before I wake up screaming, I hear the engineers talking:

Engineer #1: This solution will work, but it will be more dangerous.

Engineer #2: How much more dangerous?

Engineer #1: I figure a thousand people would die. And most of them would be strangers.

Engineer #2: Is there any way we could modify it . . . you know, to kill more strangers?

Engineer #1: Wow, you hate strangers, too?

Engineer #2: Who doesn't? Plus, I figure there's a good chance that you'd be killed doing the modifications.

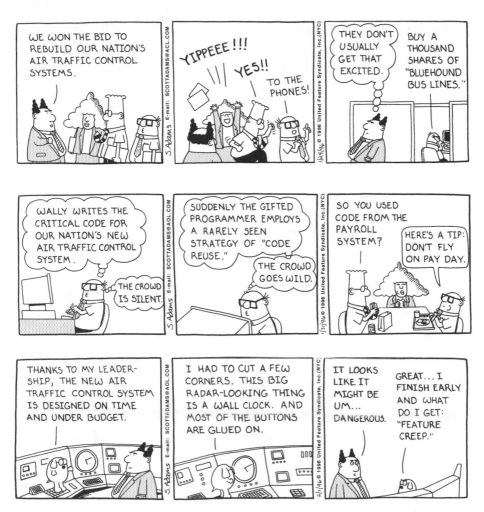

Sometimes I fear that I will forget all of my passwords and my secret codes and some large organization will keep all of my money because I can't prove it ever belonged to me. My driver's license and passport will be useless, because toddlers will have the technology to forge that kind of thing on their little "Forge-n-Learn" toys.

So one day I'll find myself in a heated argument with a banking representative in which I try to explain that I really am stupid enough to forget all of my secret codes. I won't know whether I should make an eloquent argument, thus jeopardizing my claim of stupidity, or a really stupid argument, thus proving that I'm correct about how stupid I am. It will all be terribly confusing and frustrating.

Eventually, I'll become a pathetic homeless guy, wandering around muttering, "Was it gb7k99 or was it gB7k99. I'm sure the 'B' is capitalized!"

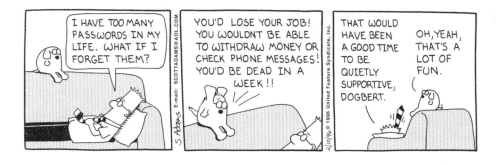

Technology also allows us to get very angry and abusive with people who can't punch us in the nose at that very minute. That is bound to be a dangerous situation, especially for scrawny vegetarians like myself. I never hesitate to question someone's parentage or offer obscene dining suggestions by e-mail. I cleverly calculate the precise amount of insult that will make someone *think* about tracking me down and beating me up, but not mad enough to actually do it. The trouble is, it's a fine line between being almost hunted down and actually hunted down. That's why I sleep in the attic most of the time and leave a dummy in my bed. (I don't call her dummy to her face. I mumble so it sounds like "honey.")

Kidding!

When it comes to physical toughness, there are two types of people:

There are people like me . . . and then there are people who can beat the crap out of people like me. The latter have always been bullies. As children, it was their responsibility to administer the wedgies and noogies to all of the other children. This taught the bullies responsibility. They learned to control their power.

Those of us who were on the receiving end of the wedgies and noogies never learned to control our power, because we didn't have any. Until now. E-mail allows us to lash out at the people we consider stupid while leaving plenty of time to run away if things get out of hand.

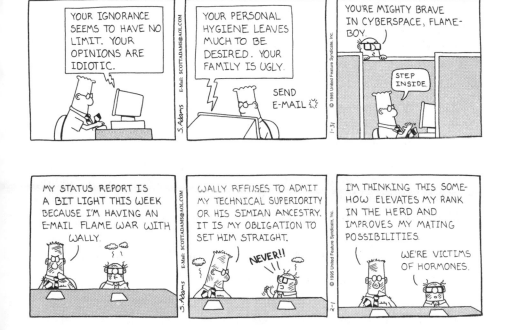

One of the biggest unreported sources of potential violence is a direct result of technology. Quite accidentally, technology has become so important that the people who control it have great power over the rest of us. Sadly, in the real world you hardly ever hear the sentence, "Not only is he great with technology, but he's a friendly person and helpful, too!" Instead, you get this guy:

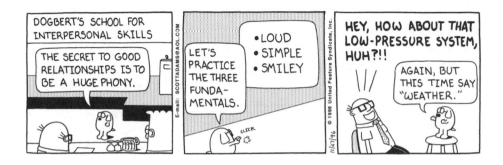

There's also a growing threat from smaller countries who have access to more technology than they can handle. I'm not just talking about nuclear devices. Undeveloped countries are interested in lots of technologies that could blow up or possibly fall on your head if you do something stupid. Imagine a world where hundreds of countries have inexpensive technology to launch huge payloads into low Earth orbits, but don't have any compelling reason to do so. This could be very dangerous.

"Hey, Borpney, what should we do with this old broken truck?"

"Let's launch it into space. (Hee hee. Snort.)"

If every little pissant country like France, for example, starts sending rockets into space, it won't be safe to come out of your basement. You'll take two steps onto your lawn and a booster rocket will crush your skull. That's no way to live.

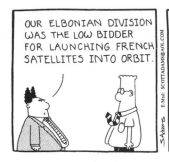

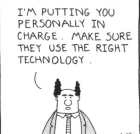

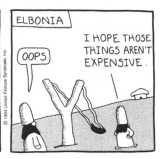

MEN WHO USE COMPUTERS—THE NEW SEX SYMBOLS

I wrote this article for the May 1995 edition of *Windows* magazine. It is reprinted here with some minor modifications. *Windows* magazine had asked me to write a column of either 700 or 1,100 words. Then they made the mistake of telling me they would pay me per word. This is what they got.

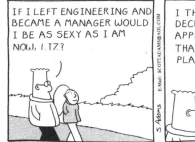

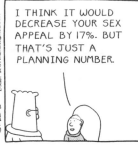

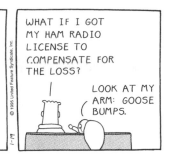

I get about 350 e-mail messages a day from readers of my comic strip *Dilbert*. Most are from disgruntled office workers, psychopaths, stalkers, comic fans—that sort of person. But a growing number are from women who write to say they think Dilbert is sexy. Some women say they already married a "Dilbert" and couldn't be happier. They gush about the virtues of their very own Dilbert.

If you're not familiar with Dilbert, he's an electrical engineer who spends most of his time with his computer. He's a nice guy, but not exactly Kevin Costner. (I'm talking about the old Kevin Costner who had good hair.)

A few years ago, I drew a *Dilbert* comic where his dog, Dogbert, put up a billboard advertising "Date a Dilbert—quantities are limited." It needed a phone number, so I used the number for my home fax, which I temporarily equipped with an answering machine in case anybody tried to call.

I got 650 calls.

Most of the calls were from men who wondered if Dilbert had a sister. Other callers wanted to fix their dog up with Dogbert. But many callers were women who said they thought Dilbert was sexy. This puzzled me.

Okay, Dilbert is polite, honest, employed, and educated. And he stays home. These are good traits, but they don't explain the incredible sex appeal.

So what's the attraction?

I think it's a Darwinian thing. We're attracted to the people who have the best ability to survive and thrive. In the old days, it was important to be able to run down an antelope and kill it with a single blow to the forehead. But that skill is becoming less important every year.

Now it only matters if you can install your own Ethernet card without having to confess your inadequacies to a disgruntled tech support person.

It's obvious that the world has three distinct classes of people, each with its own evolutionary destiny:

1. Knowledgeable computer users who will eventually evolve into godlike non-corporeal beings who rule the Universe.

2. Computer owners who try to "pass" as knowledgeable but secretly use a hand calculator to add totals for their Excel spreadsheets. This group will gravitate toward jobs as high school principals and operators of pet crematoriums. Eventually, they will become extinct.

3. Non–computer users who will eventually grow tails, sit in zoos, and fling dung at tourists.

PREDICTION 18

In the future, computer-using men will be the sexiest males.

Obviously, if you're a woman and you're trying to decide which evolutionary track you want your offspring to take, you don't want to put them on the luge ride to the dung-flinging Olympics. You want a real man. You want a knowledgeable computer user with evolutionary potential.

And women prefer men who are good listeners. Computer users are excellent listeners, because they can look at you for long periods of time without saying anything. Granted, early on in a relationship it's better if the guy actually talks, but men are not deep. We use up all the stories we'll ever have after six months. If a woman marries a guy who's in, let's say, a retail sales career, she'll get repeat stories starting in the seventh month and lasting forever. But if she marries an engineer, she gets a great listener for the next seventy years.

With the ozone layer evaporating, it's good strategy to mate with somebody who has an indoor hobby. Outdoorsy men are applying suntan lotion with SPF 10,000 and yet, by the age of thirty, they still look like dried chili peppers with pants. Compare that with the healthy glow of a man who spends twelve hours a day in front of a video screen.

And it's a well-established fact that computer users are better lovers. I know this is true, because I heard an actual anecdote from somebody who knew a woman who married a computer user. They reportedly had sex many times. I realize this isn't statistically valid, but you have to admit it's the most persuasive thing I've written so far.

If there's still any doubt in your mind about male computer users being sexier, consider their hair. Male computer users tend to have two kinds of hair:

1. Male pattern baldness—a sign of elevated testosterone.

2. Unkempt jungle hair—the kind you only see on people who have just finished a frenzied bout of lovemaking.

If this were a trial, I think we could reach a verdict on the strong circumstantial evidence alone.

I realize there are a lot of skeptics out there. They'll delight in pointing out the number of computer users who wear wrist braces, and they'll suggest it isn't the repetitive use of the keyboard that causes the problem. That's okay. Someday those skeptics will be flinging dung at tourists. Then who's laughing? (Answer to rhetorical question: everybody but the tourists.)

Henry Kissinger said power is the ultimate aphrodisiac. (This was much catchier than his original motto: "Thick glasses are the ultimate aphrodisiac.") And Bill Clinton once said that knowledge is power. Therefore, logically, according to the government of the United States, knowledge of computers is the ultimate aphrodisiac. You could argue with me—I'm just a cartoonist—but it's hard to argue with the government. Remember, they run the Bureau of Alcohol, Tobacco, and Firearms, so they must know a thing or two about satisfying women.

You might think this is enough evidence to convince anybody that men who use computers are sexy, but look at it from my point of view—I'm getting paid by the word for this article. I'm not done with you yet. Don't be so selfish.

In less enlightened times, the best way to impress women was to own a hot car. But women wised up and figured out it was better to buy their own hot cars and then they wouldn't have to ride around with jerks.

Subsequently, technology has replaced hot cars as the new symbol of robust manhood. Men instinctively know that unless they're seriously considering getting a digital line to the Internet, no woman is going to look at them twice.

And it's getting worse. In the not-too-distant future, anybody who doesn't have their own home page on the World Wide Web will probably qualify for a government subsidy for the home-pageless. And nobody likes a man who takes money from the government, except maybe Marilyn Monroe, which is why the CIA killed her. And if you think that sounds stupid, I've got about a hundred words to go.

And there's the issue of mood lighting. Good lighting is important for bringing out a person's sex appeal. And nothing looks sexier than a man in boxer shorts illuminated only by the light of a fifteen-inch SVGA monitor. Now, if we can agree that this is every woman's dream scenario, then I think we can also agree that it's best if the guy knows how to use the computer he's sitting in front of. I mean, otherwise he'll just look like a loser sitting in front of a PC in his underwear.

FOUR

LIFE ON OTHER PLANETS

There has been much speculation about whether there is life on other planets. In particular, we wonder if life on those planets is so boring that they're willing to travel thousands of light-years to stick various objects into the body holes of earthlings.

You wouldn't think a highly advanced race of beings would find that entertaining. But *we're* an advanced civilization, and there are lots of people who think cow-tipping* is a sport. Maybe we're not being visited by the cream of the alien crop, if you know what I mean. The aliens that come our way probably aren't the same bunch of aliens who invented space travel on their planets. Just look at the people driving past you on the highway; how many of them could have invented the automobile? Maybe the aliens who visit us are alien Induhviduals.

Let's not jump to any conclusions. I will use my uncanny powers of logic to ferret out the truth about UFOs and alien abductions. There's plenty of evidence to piece it all together. I don't know why no one has tried it before.

Every year, thousands of Induhviduals report sightings of flying saucers. Some of the Induhviduals have captured grainy images of these unexplained ships on video cameras. All of the alien ships filmed by Induhviduals look exactly like ashtrays or the tops of garbage pails. But what are the odds there would be that many ashtrays and garbage pail lids

---

*For you city dwellers, cow-tipping involves sneaking up on sleepy cows on hills and pushing them over so they roll down the hill. This is very bad for the cow, and it is even worse for anyone who is tired of hearing "milkshake" puns.

flying around? That seems far less likely than the explanation that the skies are filled with unidentified flying spacecrafts.

I think we can logically conclude from the video evidence that the accounts of unidentified "visitors" are true. The question is, Where did they come from?

The popular view is that the strange creatures travel from a distant planet. This assumes three things about these creatures:

1. They are capable of intergalactic travel.

2. They are capable of finding us in the vastness of space.

3. Their stealth technology makes video images of their ships look like grainy pictures of ashtrays and garbage pail lids.

This seems plausible to me, but you must compare this theory to the only logical alternative: The strange creatures live on Earth, but they are hiding most of the time.

Ask yourself this: Is it easier to build a spaceship capable of intergalactic travel or hide behind some trees? I think you can see where I'm heading with this. If not, let me back up and put it all together for you.

You might have noticed that the world is full of people who are much smarter than other people. For example, the average IQ in the general population is 100. If you remove from the sample all of the people reading this book, the average drops to maybe 40 or 45, tops. On the other end of the spectrum, Marilyn vos Savant's IQ is well over 200.

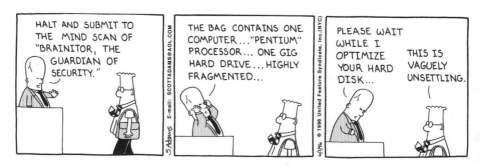

Just how big a difference is there between Marilyn vos Savant and the "average" person? Let me put it this way. Imagine that a true/false test is administered to three creatures: Marilyn vos Savant, her dog, and an average Induhvidual. Now imagine that the questions are so hard that you need an IQ of 180 or higher to do well.

Marilyn's score would be 100 percent. The Induhvidual's score would be 50 percent, assuming normal luck in guessing. Marilyn's dog would also score 50 percent, because his strategy would be no more effective than the Induhvidual's.

From Marilyn's perspective, there's not a big difference between the average Induhvidual and the dog, except the dog is cuter. Who do you think she'd rather spend time with?

There's a point coming, albeit slowly.

Throughout history, there have always been super-smart people born to the general population. I'm guessing they wouldn't want to hang around with the rest of us. Being super-smart, they'd find an alternative. They'd figure out where they could go live with each other and they'd create an elaborate cover story to keep the Induhviduals away.

If such a place existed on Earth, we could identify it with some good investigative work. All we would have to do is look for a place where all the problems caused by stupid people don't exist. I think that land would look like this:

How Super-Smart Land Would Be

> They would be neutral in all wars.
> Their clocks would be very, very accurate.
> They would have the highest standard of living.
> They would have excellent chocolate.
> Their pocketknives would be extraordinary.

Obviously, the super-smart people created their own country long ago and called it Switzerland. Every weekend, they take the hovercrafts out and look for Induhviduals who have video cameras. It's a game with them. After years of inbreeding, the super-smart people have evolved into skinny, gray creatures with huge eyes. They wear makeup to look like stern Germans when tourists are around.

PREDICTION 19

In the future, we'll realize that the creatures we thought were from other planets are actually smart people who live in Switzerland.

You might think I'm jumping to conclusions here, but have you ever met anyone from Switzerland? Neither have I.

That's my theory, and in the future you will see that I am right.

FIVE

THE WORLD GETS MORE COMPLICATED

It seems like everything I own is broken. Here is a sample of the things that are defective at the time of this writing:

Defective Things in My Home

- My online service says "try again later."

- My television won't let me look at channel 2.

- My TV remote control is broken.

- None of my telephones work.

- My stereo is blinking wildly for no reason.

- My headphones are broken.

- My computer freezes up several times a day.

- My laptop computer is broken.

- My pager only shows the tops of numbers.

- My fax line is dead.

- The timer on the water sprinkler is broken.

- My outside lights are broken.

- My roof is leaking.

- My vacuum cleaner is broken.

- My furnace is broken.

- My toilets require handle-jiggling.

- My cat needs to visit the vet.

This is not an unusual day for me. My car stopped working recently, so I bought a new one. The new one lasted approximately sixty seconds before its first major malfunction—the climate control computer failed as I pulled out of the dealer's lot. I was surprised, because I expected to make it all the way to the intersection before something like that happened.

Now, only a few weeks later, I have a new car problem. A light on the dashboard says, "Check Engine." What does that mean? I looked under the hood, and the engine is still there. That wasn't enough to make the light go out. I need another hint.

I feel helpless around all of my broken stuff. I can't fix *anything* myself. There's a blown lightbulb at the highest point of my ceiling. I can't figure out how to change it. I don't have a ladder that goes that high. Even if I did, I wouldn't want to risk my life to change a lightbulb. I'd hate to die changing a lightbulb, because that's how everyone would remember me. Nobody would say, "I'll miss him." They'd say, "How many cartoonists does it take to change a lightbulb? Ha ha ha!" If I'm going to die in a household accident, I want it to be one that doesn't involve lightbulbs.

The hardware store has a device for changing lightbulbs. It's a long pole with a lightbulb grabber on the end. It says on the instructions that it only works if you had originally put the lightbulb in with that sort of device. How should I know what the previous owner used to put that lightbulb in with? He could have used a trained monkey taped to a broom, for all I know. If I buy this bulb-changer device, I will end up beating the lightbulb senseless, getting amazingly frustrated, and gaining nothing in terms of illumination. And it will take the entire afternoon to fail at this task.

I can't solve the lightbulb problem myself. How do I find someone who changes lightbulbs for a living? Do I check the Yellow Pages under the letter "T" for "Tall Guy Who Changes Lightbulbs"? Or how about "S" for "Someone Who Isn't a Total Loser Like Me"?

I am totally stumped by this lightbulb dilemma. I use my flashlight if I want to see anything at night in that room. I plan to move my broken stereo in there, because the blinking lights will act like a night-light. If that's not enough, I always have the sound of my running toilets to act as a homing beacon.

I live in a crumbling and defective world. I'm too busy or too clueless to fix any of it. It wouldn't help anyway. As soon as I fixed one thing, another thing would sense the void and plunge into spontaneous disrepair. At least with my method—the "Active Neglect" method—I can show off my nice things to friends and still be free from the maintenance.

"That's my stereo in that dark room over there. No, you can't listen to it, but you can see it when it blinks."

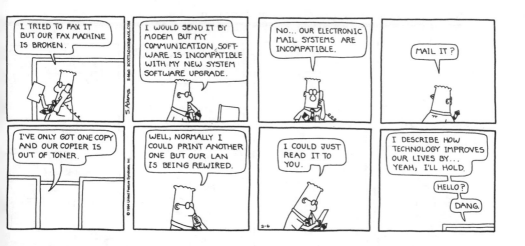

Other futurists predict the world will become increasingly polarized into technology "haves" and "have-nots." The part they get wrong is that the "have-nots" will be the lucky ones.

The "have-nots" won't spend hours a day trying to keep their stuff working. They'll be sitting on the porch sipping lemonade and whittling little animals to give away as gifts. Meanwhile, I'll be trying to figure out why I can't get five peripherals to work on my SCSI chain. And I'll be doing it in the dark.

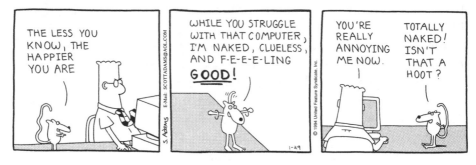

We techno-buried people will envy the rocking chairs of the simple people. We'll thirst for their lemonade. And we'll hate the little carved animals they keep giving us on special occasions (although I won't mind them too much if I can burn them for heat and light).

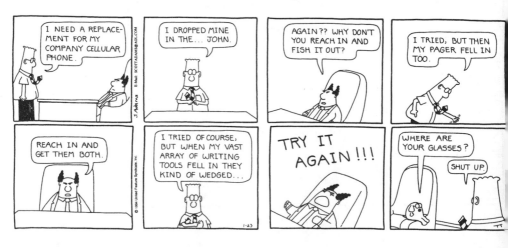

This movement toward simplification has already started, but it won't get huge until the simple-life people have their own magazine called *LoafWeek* with a bunch of blank pages. They will have their own television show featuring a guy sitting in a chair doing nothing. The show won't be broadcast in the traditional sense, since none of the target audience will own televisions, but people will enjoy knowing there's a guy sitting in a chair someplace at the same time every week.

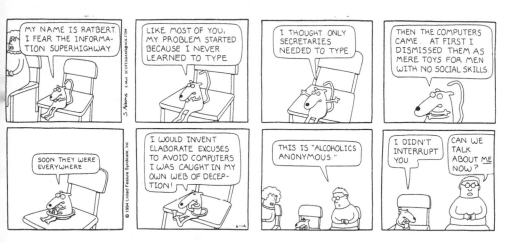

People who cling to their complicated lifestyles will be willing to pay anything to have other people do the things they don't have the time or skill to do themselves. Many people already pay for housecleaning, cooking (at restaurants), changing the oil in the car, and mowing the lawn.

PREDICTION 20

In the future, the trend of "personal services" will continue until busy people are handling almost none of their routine bodily functions themselves.

I saw a glimpse of the future recently when I had a cameo appearance on the TV show *NewsRadio*. Between takes, a makeup expert would swoop in and dab some makeup on my shiny forehead and wet down the only scrap of hair I have, which tragically happens to be a cowlick. How great it would be to have people swoop in and straighten you up during the day. They could shadow you from morning to night, always ready to charge in and knock an eyelash off your cheek or zip up your pants if you forgot.

A professional photographer was nice enough to send me some photos from a public talk I did recently. The photos clearly showed a huge chunk of food stuck in my teeth during my presentation. I wish someone had swooped in and saved me from that embarrassment. I would have paid a lot for that service. Ideally, this person would be someone petite whom I could tape to a broomstick to change my lightbulbs. But that's just dreaming.

THE INCOMPETENCE LINE

Every year, it takes more brains to navigate this complicated world. More people are falling below what I call the "incompetence line," through no fault of their own.

I fell below the incompetence line this year. I use airline travel as my benchmark. Air travel has become amazingly complicated. The percentage of the population that is too dumb to fly gets bigger every day.

Imagine if you had never traveled by air and you had to figure it out without asking anyone for help. You would have many questions that do not have intuitive answers:

Nonintuitive Air Travel Questions

- Should you put your arms around the person in front of you and lean into the curves?
- How much should you tip the flight attendants?
- How many times can you go through the metal detector before you become sterile?

- Are the skycaps authorized to do strip searches or are they just kidding about that?

I used to think I had all of the air travel questions figured out. I felt like quite the accomplished traveler. I learned that I have to order my vegetarian meals twenty-four hours in advance so they have more time to forget it. I learned to avoid the last row on the plane, because the seat doesn't lean back. I know just how much reading material to bring for the flight. I even got luggage with built-in wheels so I don't have to prove to the world that I haven't been to the gym lately. For a while, I was comfortably above the incompetence line for air travel.

Then the frequent flyer programs started kicking in. Suddenly, the airlines began sending weekly envelopes stuffed full of offers for hotels, luggage, rental cars, and free trips. All I had to do was use their airline and then figure out how their reward program worked. I would be awash in free stuff. Woo-hoo!

But it didn't work out that way. Instead, my spare bedroom and three file cabinets are packed full of complicated literature from the airlines. I keep telling myself I'll look at it closely and figure it all out "in my free time," but every day a truck pulls up to my house and dumps another load of airline literature on my lawn. It has miles of fine print about things like black-out periods and award levels and expiration dates and special offers. According to the airlines, I'm an executive something and a gold something and a frequent something, all of which gives me many rights and privileges—if I just had time to figure out what they are.

Then the airlines started ganging up with hotels and credit card companies to increase the complexity. I believe I have millions of dollars worth of unclaimed prizes now, if only I could figure out where they are and how to claim them.

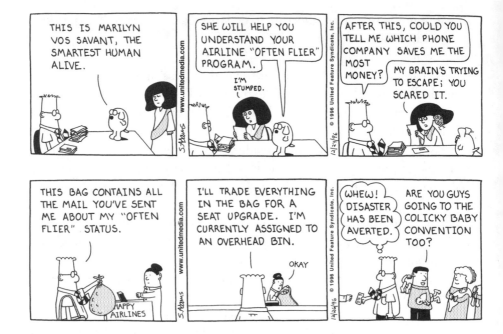

So I am now officially below the incompetence line when it comes to flying. I can still figure out how to fly from one place to the next, but I'm sure I'm doing it wrong. By wrong, I mean that I'm spending more money and getting less free stuff than I could if I were smarter. But I don't have time to be smarter. I can't dedicate my life to my airline reward programs. The airlines have defeated me. I am buried under mounds of good news from them. They have pushed me below the incompetence line for their service and I don't like it one bit.

I don't think I'm alone. Other people must be getting forced below the incompetence line every day. Some people don't have so far to go. I get especially scared when the flight attendant is reading the safety instructions and I glance at the Induhviduals sitting in the escape-door aisles. I'm quite certain that if the plane had an emergency, these people would grab the headphones out of the seat-back pockets, hold them to their mouths, and try to breathe. Other people would run into the rest rooms and try to flush themselves to safety. If you could put on special goggles that allowed you to identify which people around you are below the incompetence line already, it would be truly frightening, especially if you were near a reflective surface.

This all brings me to my prediction.

PREDICTION 21

Lack of education will not be the biggest problem in the future. The problem will be an excess of stupidity as more people fall below the incompetence line.

I don't want to come off sounding like one of those conspiracy nuts, but I'm fairly sure everything in my house was designed by someone who is intentionally trying to kill me or make me feel stupid.

I think it might be this guy:

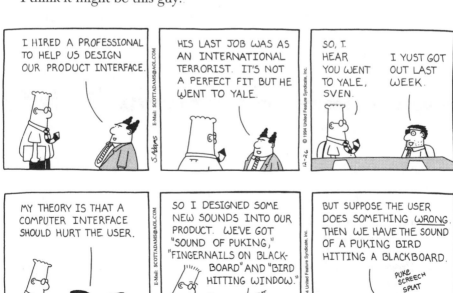

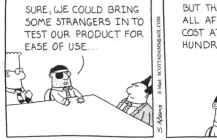
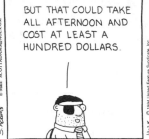
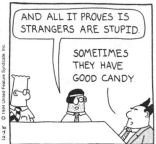

When I was a kid, I had a little black-and-white Sears television set that was very easy to use. There were only three steps:

1. Turn on power.

2. Select channel.

3. Wrap a long string to the horizontal hold knob on the side of the television so I could continually adjust it from across the room by pulling the string with my feet.

Those simple days are gone. Now I have a home entertainment center. It has six remote controls. If I want to watch television using the satellite dish as a source, I follow these steps:

1. Hire Sherpa guides.

2. Mount expedition to locate the AVR 80 remote control.

3. Press the "Main Power" button. (If nothing happens, unplug and replug TV set.)

4. Press the "LD" button. (LD stands for "satellite dish." Don't ask why.)

5. Press the "Source Power" button.

6. Switch to RCA remote control.

7. Press "Guide" button.

8. Scroll to movie *Broken Arrow*.

9. Press "Display."

10. Press "Menu-Select."

There are lots of other buttons on my remote controls. They have names like Fetch, Matrix, DISC DECK ANT, FAV•INPUT, and MEMO. I don't trust myself with this much power. I'm afraid I'll hit the wrong button and turn off the life support systems on the Russian space station. I don't want that on my conscience, so I leave those buttons alone.

The satellite dish has added a lot to my viewing pleasure. For example, I can watch the movie *Broken Arrow* at just about any time of day for only three dollars. I've seen it 700 times so far. There are other movies, too, but they don't interest me. I don't want to feel like the system is a waste of money, so I watch *Broken Arrow* whenever I can.

You can also watch sports from all over the country, with the exception of your local teams, which are blacked out. This is handy if you're traveling, but only if you're willing to take your dish with you and install it in your hotel room. That's the only way you're going to see your favorite team, no matter where you are.

You can't beat the picture clarity on a satellite system. It won't help you with any of the network television shows, because you can't get those on the dish, for some legal reason, unless you live in the wilderness. But you can watch the *Howard Stern* radio show on E! channel. I think it's important to have full digital clarity when you're watching a radio show. I already forget how I lived without it.

I used to know how to record television shows on my VCR. I had a success rate of well over 60 percent, which I believe put me in the ninety-fifth percentile of the general population. But that was when I had a television set, not a home entertainment center. Now I can't figure out how to record anything. My success rate is 0 percent and holding. I have fallen below the incompetence line in entertainment. I am now literally too dumb to entertain myself.

All day long, my television set powers itself on and off randomly. It does this to tease me. I believe it is on the verge of becoming a sentient life-form. ("Sentient" is a word I learned from watching *Star Trek* episodes back when I knew how to use the television, before my *Broken Arrow* days.)

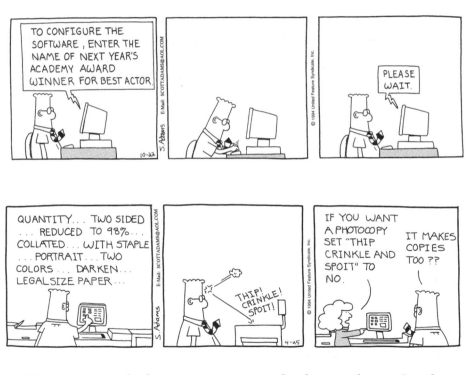

It's tempting to think we can compensate for the complexity of modern life by improving the educational system, but it won't help me unless there's an evening degree program in watching television. Education isn't the fix-all solution everyone wants it to be. There are only two types of educations:

1. Useful.

2. Useless.

If you're foolish enough to get one of those useful educations, such as an engineering degree, everything you learn will be obsolete in five years. The rest of what you learn for the remainder of your life will come from reading brochures from vendors.

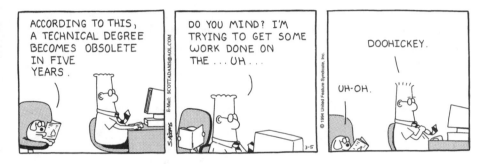

That's why I majored in economics. With economics, you never have to worry that your degree will become less relevant over time. I mean, how the hell could it?

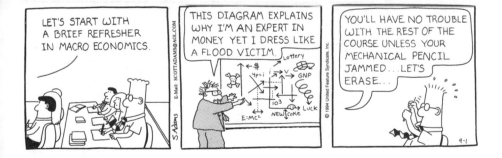

I tried to use my economics training at my first job out of college. I was a bank teller. I soon found my knowledge more of a burden than an advantage. My co-workers were happily taking deposits and earning money for the bank. Meanwhile, I would be explaining to my customers how they should empty their passbook savings accounts and invest in small cap mutual funds through a discount brokerage company. Ironically, the more I displayed my knowledge of economics, the less money I earned in raises.

My economics degree wasn't enough to help me as a bank teller. Stupidity is immune to education. We're being buried by the growing complexity of the world—which makes us stupider every day—and we have no strategy for survival.

Our only hope in the future is that a charismatic figure will emerge and rid the world of creeping, sadistic complexity before it's too late. Maybe it will be Dogbert.

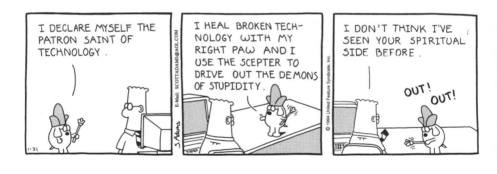

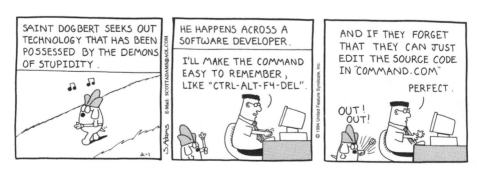

YOUR BUSY LIFE

What's the future look like? I'll tell you: It's about tough choices. For example, this morning I noticed that my electric razor had spilled its entire collection of whiskers all over the inside of my fashionable leather toiletry bag. I had two choices. I could laboriously remove those whiskers, individually cleaning each of the other contents of the bag, thus missing at least an hour of useful work, or I could say to myself, "If I didn't mind having those whiskers on my face, why should I mind them on my little traveling aspirin bottle?"

I chose the latter. After all, I already got used to the toothpaste all over everything in that bag. How bad could a few hairs be?

That's what the future looks like—a bag filled with toothpaste, whiskers, and unidentified containers. We're entering an age when the things we need to do and want to do are absorbed and overwhelmed by other things we need to do and want to do. We'll make random, often stupid choices, because we don't have the brains or time to do better.

Our only hope is that the marketplace will work its magic and provide the services that busy people need to get by. That seems to be happening.

PREDICTION 22

In the future, there will be a huge increase in the number of "household services" to compensate for the pathetic incompetence of the average person.

HOUSEHOLD SERVICES

Every year, I'm becoming a bit more helpless when it comes to maintaining my house. I depend on "service people" to come over and do two vital things in my house:

1. Fix something.

2. Make me feel like a complete loser.

Household Service people use even more confusing language than people who work in big companies. At least the jargon in big companies is a language that can be understood by a few people in the department. Service people, on the other hand, seem to develop their unique language while driving around in their trucks all alone. As far as I can tell, the language is some combination of traffic noises, bodily emanations, and snippets from talk radio all rolled into one. I had a service person install some telephone wiring in my house recently, and a conversation with him went like this:

Wire guy:	The line loops to the outside patch then goes live from the cable to the scromet.
Me:	What's a scromet? And which line are you talking about?
Wire guy:	That's what patches into the live cable wire from the blue wires, unless you want it to be the orange ones. It's up to you.
Me:	Why would I care what color the wire is? And what the hell is a scromet?
Wire guy:	Okay, we'll go with the blue. But don't complain later when you wish you'd said orange.
Me:	Why? Why orange? What's the difference? And what's a scromet?
Wire guy:	The scromet is connected to the orange directly. That's my point.

Me: YOUR *POINT*?! I DON'T UNDERSTAND A
                   WORD YOU'RE SAYING. WHAT POINT??

Wire guy: So, we'll go with the blue wire. I'm sure you
                   know best.

So now my scromet is wired to something or other and all I know is that every time the phone rings my shower comes on. I'd call the wire guy back to have it fixed, but I can't go through that experience again.

SIX

THE FUTURE OF DEMOCRACY AND CAPITALISM

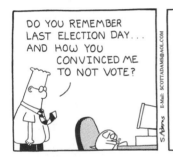
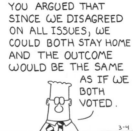
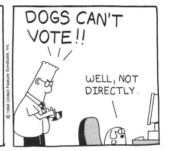

On election day, I always perform my civic duty by not voting. Believe me, the country is better off if I stay away from the polls. I am far too ignorant to add anything but randomness to the outcome. I say this despite the fact that I read as many bumper stickers as I can, thus making me more informed than the average voter.

Even if I were uncaring enough to participate in elections, I wouldn't know how to register without exposing myself to unnecessary risk. Someone told me I can go to the post office to register, but I'm afraid they'll throw my application in the wrong bag and I'll end up in the military. The next thing I know, I'm a Navy SEAL. I'm fairly certain I would be killed by my own squad in order to put an end to my incessant seal puns.

I realize it's a small risk, but when I compare it to the statistical likelihood that my vote will improve the efficiency of our government, I think it's a fair assessment. And when you factor in the odds of being hit by a stray bullet while standing in line at the post office, voting seems downright reckless. My cats need me alive, despite any outward signs to the contrary, such as dragging me into the litter box and covering me with sand.

When it comes to voting, I'm just barely smart enough to know that I'm a total idiot. This might sound self-deprecating, but on the intelligence scale, it puts me comfortably ahead of all the Induhviduals who actually vote.

To understand how voting became a futile exercise, let me give you a refresher course on early American history. A few hundred years ago in early America, a bunch of intelligent, hard-working landowners set out to design a new form of government that emphasized fairness. They came up with a system that favored intelligent, hard-working landowners. There were bonus points for being a "dorky white male."

There was a heated discussion among the Founding Fathers about the wisdom of openly discriminating against everyone else, especially the stupid white males (let's call them, collectively, the pre-Induhviduals). There were so many of them, and they all had weapons. This fear was allayed when Benjamin Franklin pointed out, "Hey, they're pre-Induhviduals. The worst thing that could happen is they'll get mad at us and try to attack France." Everyone laughed so hard the floor was covered with wooden dentures. It took hours to sort it out.

During the cocktail hour afterward, some of the Founding Fathers questioned Ben about his use of the phrase "pre-Induhviduals," pointing out that the term "Induhviduals" hadn't been created yet. Ben just smiled and mumbled something about being ahead of his time. Then he got in his car and drove home.

Declaring independence wasn't enough. There was still the small matter of breaking free from England. The Founding Fathers created a fighting force of pre-Induhviduals and ordered them to kill everyone in the British army. We have no information about the Induhvidualness of the British soldiers except that they wore bright red uniforms and marched on unprotected roads in good lighting while singing the British fight song that goes like this: "Shoot me . . . shoot me . . . shoot me." (For a more complete discussion of this phenomenon, refer to Charles Darwin's *The Origin of Species*.) Eventually, this tedious war was over and America was born.

Long after the Founding Fathers laughed themselves to death, the original intent of the Constitution was forgotten and the bonus points for being a dorky white guy were removed from the law. But the core of the system—giving the shaft to lazy and stupid people who have no land (or "capital")—remained intact, forming the basis of our capitalist system. It has worked very well so far.

Any kind of system will tend to discriminate against one group or another. The beauty of our current system of capitalism is that it legally discriminates against the two groups who are least likely to complain: stupid people, AKA Induhviduals, because they don't realize they're getting screwed; and lazy people, because protesting is like work. Unlike other forms of discrimination that are rightly outlawed, almost everyone agrees it's fair to discriminate against lazy and stupid people. It's a very stable system.

PREDICTION 23

Democracy and capitalism will continue to give the shaft to lazy and stupid people. Neither group will complain.

Despite their many shortcomings, Induhviduals and lazy people often end up with large amounts of money through a variety of nonproductive activities, including inheritance, marriage, lotteries, crime, and middle management. In the future, you can expect rapid growth in any business that seeks to take money from Induhviduals and lazy people. Here are some good industries for investment:

- Television.

- Hair growth shampoos.

- Stretch pants.

- Home exercise equipment.

THE FUTURE OF VOTING

In the early days of the United States, it made sense to let ordinary people vote. The issues were relatively simple ones that anyone could understand.

Example of Simple Political Issue from the Past

"Do you think our national bird should be the bald eagle or the turkey?"

Anyone could have an informed opinion on that issue. You could be the kind of guy who's out in the barn trying to milk the chickens and you'd still have all the brainpower needed to cast a meaningful vote on the national bird question.

Thankfully, the voters chose wisely on the national bird issue. Otherwise we'd have to insult people by calling them eagles. Boy Scouts would aspire to be Turkeys. I wouldn't want to live in that country.

Lately, the issues have become so complicated that the average voter is totally baffled. There aren't any simple bird-related questions anymore. It's all complicated stuff like economic policies, strategic alliances, and national health care. The average citizen can't possibly spend enough time to have informed opinions on those subjects, but the country hums right along anyway, because a total lack of comprehension doesn't stop people from having strong opinions and "voting their conscience."

If you think I'm overstating the case, try this exercise. Keep a completely straight face and ask several registered voters this question.

Voter Comprehension Question

"Do you think the Federal Reserve should increase the money supply or should they be required to wear school uniforms?"

The question makes no sense, but I'll bet you can find someone who has a strong opinion about it. Humans have become so accustomed to forming opinions about things they don't understand that it's almost a reflex.

You might be thinking that I'm being overly dismissive of the average person's ability to grasp complicated issues. Here is a true story about an average person, sent to me by a *Dilbert* reader:

True Story of an Average Person

A secretary was asked to order paper for the office fax machine. The need was immediate, and she didn't want to wait for the next-day delivery. Thinking "outside the box," she called the office supply store and asked if they would fax her some paper to hold them over until the delivery came.

How much should we cut taxes to stimulate the economy without causing inflation? Let's ask the secretary who's waiting for some paper to be faxed to her!

The worst invention in the democratic world is something called referendums. That's where the voters get to vote directly for something. The proponents of most referendums are either intentionally trying to mislead the voters or too stupid to explain the issues clearly. Take a look at this recent true example I received by e-mail:

From: (name deleted)
To: scottadams@aol.com

Last month the South Carolina ballot contained a referendum question so that each county could decide whether their "blue laws" should be abolished. These are the laws that control when businesses may open on Sundays. Charleston and Greenville had already abolished their Sunday blue laws, but other counties had not.

The exact wording of the referendum follows.

"Shall the prohibition on Sunday work continue in this county subject to an employee's right to elect not to work on Sunday if the prohibition is not continued after certification of the result of this referendum to the Secretary of State?"

In the case of Greenville County voters, a "no" vote meant they wanted Greenville County to be exempt from the blue laws (which it already was), and a "yes" vote meant they wanted to put the blue laws back into effect in Greenville County.

So many voters misinterpreted what "continue" and "continued" meant in the question that they voted "yes." The blue laws will probably be reinstated here in Greenville County.

If voters have opinions but don't have knowledge or comprehension of the issues, what are they basing their opinions on?

You don't want to know.

Nineteen of the last twenty-six U.S. presidential elections were won by the taller candidate. I know that's true, because I heard it on television. In the few cases where the short candidate won, he tended to have the best hair (Kennedy versus Nixon, for example). Actually, I don't know if the hair correlation is true—I just made it up—but I'd bet on it.

Prior to the Republican convention in 1996, Bob Dole was trailing Bill Clinton in the polls by double digits. Immediately following the convention, the candidates were only a few points apart. Yet the convention generated no new information for voters. No new policies were introduced. No new arguments were made. Apparently, many voters were influenced by SOMETHING other than information.

Look at the effectiveness of television campaign ads. Every voter knows that campaign ads are intentionally misleading, yet campaign ads are very effective. Often they determine the outcome of the election. Here again, people allow themselves to be influenced by something that can't be considered "information" by any stretch of the imagination.

Then there's party loyalty. No matter what information is available about the candidates, most people end up voting for the party they belong to. They remain loyal even if their party's track record and platform change. I'm convinced that if one of the major parties nominated a bag of lettuce for president, the lettuce would get 25 percent of the popular vote. This 25 percent would rationalize their decision by saying things like:

- "Well, at least that lettuce has principles!"
- "It can't be any worse than the other guy."
- "I just think it's time for a change."

Of all the things that influence elections, it appears that information is the least significant. Elections are won by the candidate whose staff members are the most skilled at manipulating the voters. That's not necessarily a bad thing, because you have to be quite smart to figure out the best way to manipulate millions of Induhviduals into marching in the same direction. And if we get tall presidents with good hair who hire smart staff members, that's not the worst thing that could happen.

PREDICTION 24

In the future, most democratic countries will be led by tall people with good hair and smart staff members.

VOTE DEFLATION

Two hundred years ago, there were only sixteen people in the whole United States who voted in the presidential election. (This is an approximation based on the assumption that I don't want to look up the real number.) If you were one of the sixteen people, your vote counted as 6.25 percent of the total votes.

If you voted in the most recent election, your vote was watered down by tens of millions of dolts who think the Speaker of the House is part of their Surround Sound stereo system. Every time a new Induhvidual is registered, the value of your vote is diluted.

PREDICTION 25

In the future, the value of your vote will become less than zero. That happens when the amount you pay in taxes to have your own vote counted is less than the value you get from the vote itself.

The crossover point is rapidly approaching. It will be much worse when technology makes it easier to register and vote.

Eventually, you will be able to vote over the Internet using your television set and remote control. This raises the frightening specter of millions of people watching *Beavis and Butt-head* and voting during the commercials. The easier it is to vote, the lower the average intelligence of the voters will be. I can't prove this, but under the current system, I have to think a lot of voters get lost on the way to the polling booth. That weeds a lot of Induhviduals out. In the future, you'll never be too drunk or too stupid to vote.

A Phrase You'll Hear in the Future

"I might be too drunk to find the polling place, but I can still help determine the future of the free world!"

Will election results be worse when we have dumber average voters? Let me walk you through a hypothetical situation. Imagine that somehow you find the 100 smartest humans on earth (Hint: look in Switzerland). You ask them to vote on an issue in which the general public is evenly divided.

There are two potential outcomes:

1. The smart people will be just as divided as the general public. That means intelligence is irrelevant to democracy. Ouch.

2. The smart people would all vote for the same side of the issue. That would indicate that intelligence is *very* relevant, but democracy erases its impact. Ouch again.

In either case, you'd find out something you really don't want to know. The scariest result would be to find out that intelligence made a big difference, because tomorrow the super-smart people will be back in Switzerland and the real elections will instead be determined by huge numbers of Induhviduals.

Given all these problems with democracy, the question for any good citizen is clear: How can I make some money out of this? It's easy.

Months before a presidential election, you will hear predictions about stocks that will be helped if a particular national candidate gets elected. For example, if one candidate opposes restrictions on tobacco companies, you might expect tobacco stocks to go up if that candidate gets elected. Having read this book, you are at an advantage compared to other investors. You know there is a 76 percent chance that the tallest candidate will be elected president. And if the tallest candidate also has the best hair, it's a mortal lock. You know which way those tobacco stocks are heading months ahead of the ignorant investors who are studying the so-called "fundamentals."

THE RISE OF THE HAIRY REASONERS

Today, if you're a stunned and confused citizen—and who isn't—you have two choices regarding voting:

Current Voting Choices

1. Make uninformed choices because it's all too confusing.

2. Be a bad citizen.

I think everyone has a nagging feeling that democracy has some bugs, but there's a complete vacuum of ideas about how to fix it. Fortunately, nature abhors a vacuum, which I assume is the reason my vacuum cleaner doesn't work. (Ironically, it does not suck.) I predict the vacuum will be filled by what I call the "Hairy Reasoners."

In the future, voters will wish that some well-informed smart person would just tell them who and what to vote for. That way citizens won't feel like their vote is a waste of time. I predict that this need will be filled with what I will call Hairy Reasoners, so called because I imagine them as people with good reasoning skills and bad hair. (People with good reasoning skills tend to have bad hair. Nobody knows why.)

PREDICTION 26

In the future, voters will be so baffled that they'll want smart people with bad hair to tell them what to do.

I expect the first Hairy Reasoners will be professors, lawyers, and judges—people who are trained to explain things logically even when it differs from their personal opinions. The Hairy Reasoners will have the rare ability to explain complex issues with logic and simple common sense.

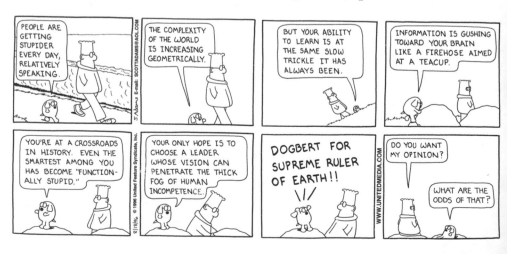

It's tempting to think voters can be educated to make better decisions on their own, but some of the dumbest things ever spoken have come out of the mouths of educated people. Well-informed, educated people need Hairy Reasoners, too.

Consider the debate about whether repeat criminals should be locked up for life. I've heard educated people argue that crime does not decrease if you keep the people who commit the crimes in jail. The people who have this opinion need someone like a Hairy Reasoner to explain the situation slowly:

"People . . . who . . . are . . . in . . . prison . . . are . . . not . . . elsewhere . . . at . . . the . . . same . . . time . . . committing . . . crimes. It's a physical law. It's math. This is not a gray area. The real issues are cost and justice."

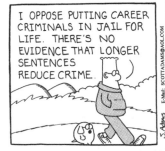 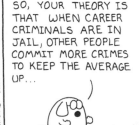 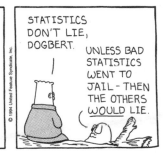

With the rise of Hairy Reasoners, democracies will experience a decade in which good judgment and informed opinions influence government. People will feel that their vote has regained its lost value. But after a few years of that nonsense, large companies will realize that it doesn't take much money to bribe a Hairy Reasoner. Then we'll see Hairy Reasoners wearing beer company shirts and explaining why it's a good idea for every citizen to smoke three packs of cigarettes a day. But it will be nice until then.

SEVEN

THE FUTURE OF GENDER RELATIONS

SEX IN THE FUTURE

Scientists tend to put the most energy into the areas that interest them personally. That makes it easy to predict one upcoming scientific breakthrough:

PREDICTION 27

In the future, scientists will create a powerful and legal aphrodisiac.

I base this prediction on the fact that most scientists are horny, heterosexual men. What do *you* think they're working on?

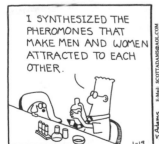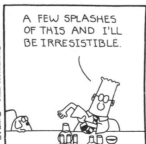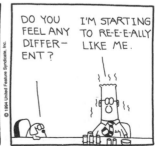

Arousal is a function of chemicals in the body. Scientists are getting very good at controlling those chemicals. Before long, we'll have a good idea exactly which chemicals cause which reactions. And since horniness is a naturally occurring condition, it will have no side effects, except for high online service charges.

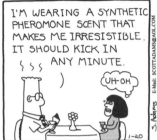
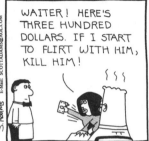
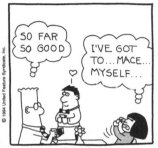

The scientists will be clever enough to disguise their discovery so it can be approved by the FDA and become widely available. I predict that the new aphrodisiac will be marketed as an antidepressant. That's not too much of a stretch, because it's difficult to be horny and sad at the same time.

The beauty of calling the aphrodisiac drug an antidepressant is that anyone can act depressed, thus qualifying for the drug. It's not as if your doctor is going to tickle you to see if you're lying. And if she does, you might want to see if her diploma is signed.

The warning on the antidepressant drug's label will say something like, "Might cause amazingly high levels of arousal. Avoid alcohol, vacuum cleaners, and farm animals."

No other marketing will be necessary.

Unfortunately, new sexually transmitted diseases will keep springing up every year. We'll have a population of incredibly horny people who are afraid to have sex with one another.

The solution is virtual reality.

Virtual reality technology is also being developed primarily by horny males. You might notice a pattern in these technical developments. Historically, the true purpose of every invention is disguised.

INVENTION	REAL PURPOSE
Club	Seduce women
Fire	Stay warm while seducing women
Printing press	Print Bibles in order to impress women
Automobile	Go on dates with women
Television	Look at women who are prettier than the ones in your house
VCR	Watch other people seduce women
Virtual reality	Imagine what it's like to seduce women

Women are largely oblivious to this scientific motivation, and that's probably a good thing. It gives women more time to run the world. That leads to my next subject, almost by coincidence.

WOMEN IN CHARGE

> ### PREDICTION 28
> In the future, women will run the world in all democratic countries.

I base this prediction on two facts that cannot be disputed:

1. Women already control the world.

2. Who's going to stop them?

Men live in a fantasy world. I know this because I am one, and I actually receive my mail there. We men like to think we're in charge because most of the top jobs in business and government are held by men, but I have a shocking statistical insight for you men—THOSE ARE *OTHER* MEN. The total percentage of men in those top spots is roughly .0000001 percent of the male population. I'm not one of them. I just draw cartoons and write these stupid books. Chances are, if you're a man reading this, you're not running the world, either.

I have about as much in common with the CEO of a Fortune 500 company as I have with my cat. It's not logical to say that I, as a man, run the world based on the fact that total strangers with similar chromosomes have excellent jobs. Yet that is exactly what many people believe.

When the Joint Chiefs of Staff are deciding whether to go to war, they do not call my house and say, "We're calling all the men who run the world to ask for their input." Believe it or not, they make those decisions without consulting me. That's probably a good thing, because I favor air strikes against all countries whose names are difficult to pronounce. It's not a "policy" in the strictest sense of the word, but it would sure make it easier to discuss world events.

Furthermore, tiny countries should have short names so the mapmakers can fit it all in. I think that would stimulate the economy somehow. But these excellent ideas are wasted under the current system of global decision-making.

Someone might argue that men have access to the top jobs whereas women do not. There's some truth to that, but the mathematical fact is, 99.9999999 percent of all men can't get those top jobs, either. There aren't enough of those jobs to go around. The rest of us men live in a world that is ruled by women, as I will explain for those of you who hadn't noticed.

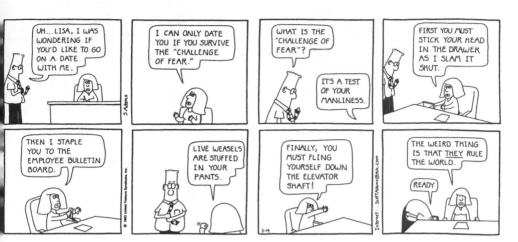

What evidence do I have that women rule the world? Take a look at the world and ask yourself how it would be different if men were REALLY in charge. Look at the things that men want most, then check to see if the world is organized to *provide* those things or to *limit* them. Logically, if men made the rules, the world would be organized to provide them with the things they want most.

Men want sex. If men ruled the world, they could get sex anywhere, anytime. Restaurants would give you sex instead of breath mints on the way out. Gas stations would give sex with every fill-up. Banks would give sex to anyone who opened a checking account.

But it doesn't work that way, at least not at my bank. (Having your own "personal banker" isn't all it's cracked up to be.)

Instead, for the most part, sex is provided by women if they feel like it, which they usually don't. If a heterosexual guy wants sex, he has to hold doors, buy flowers, act polite, lift heavy objects, kill spiders, pretend to be interested in boring things, and generally act like a complete wuss. Can anyone think men designed *that* system?

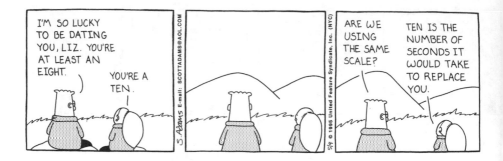

If men were smart enough to figure out what's going on, they might be tempted to use their superior size and strength to dominate women. But women are too clever to let that happen. Thousands of years ago, women figured out they could disguise their preferences as "religion" and control gullible men that way. In one part of the world, I imagine the conversation went like this:

Husband: I'll be back in an hour. I'm going to go covet my neighbor's wife.

Wife: You can't do that.

Husband: Why not?

Wife (thinking fast): Um . . . God said so. He's an omnipotent being. If you don't obey him you'll burn in hell.

Husband: Whoa, that was a close one. Thanks for warning me . . . How about if I kill her husband first?

Wife: Ooh, bad news on that, too.

PREDICTION 29

In the future, religious groups will get mad at me, thus
boosting my book sales.

Religion is only one of the ways women control men. It runs much
deeper than that. I'll explain it all in this next section.

Manners

Our lives are guided by annoying little rules called "manners." The rules
kick in whenever there are other people around, which is most of the time.
That means whoever invented these manners is controlling our behavior
most of the time without even being there.

Do you think men invented manners?

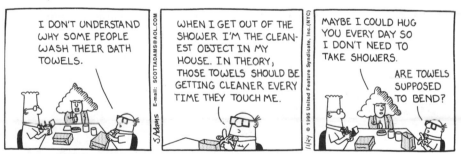

Manners would be a lot different if men created them. For example,
the Swiss Army Knife would be the right utensil for any occasion, including holidays and weddings. If you're wearing clothes, you have all you
need in the napkin department. It's that simple.

The best evidence that women invented manners is the fact that formal
dinners have many forks. This multiple-fork situation must have been
invented by people who really, really *like* forks. There's no other explanation. I have never seen a man comment on the quality or beauty of a fork.
No man ever said, "This fork is terrific. I wish I had several of them for

this meal. We can use one to eat food and the other to . . . um . . . eat more food."

If men had invented forks there would be no prohibition about using one in each hand at the same time. Obviously, women are the driving force behind the proliferation of forks, and, by logical extension, they must be responsible for all manner of manners.

We can test this assumption by looking at some of the major categories of manners and asking how likely it is that men were involved in their design.

Elbows on Table

People who have good manners don't put their elbows on the dinner table. Clearly this is not a male idea. That table is EXACTLY WHERE THE ELBOWS SHOULD GO. It makes no sense to put a table in front of a person at elbow-height if it's just going to tease. Your lap will hold a plate, but your lap won't rest your elbows. There must be some reason tables were invented. When I look at the tables in my house, they are covered with flower centerpiece thingies, but no elbows. Whose idea do you think that was? If you ask me, flowers belong in the ground and elbows belong on the table. But nobody asked.

Covering Your Sneeze

Do you think men came up with the concept of covering your mouth with your hand when you sneeze? I can't imagine a man sitting around saying, "You know, the very best place to sneeze is on part of my own body."

I don't think so. Sneezing on your own body is the very worst place you could possibly sneeze. Even your family pet knows to sneeze on a family member instead of its own paw.

Swearing

Certain words are considered impolite. Can you imagine a smoke-filled room where silver-haired men discuss which words will be considered impolite?

Smoke-Filled Room Fantasy Scene

"The next word for consideration is 'pud.'"

A collective gasp fills the room. A man in the front faints. The group wisely decides to add it to their forbidden list.

No, I can't imagine it either.

Courtship

Under our current system of courtship, men do most of the date-asking and women get to squish men's fragile egos like Fudgsicles on a Los Angeles freeway. I'm reasonably certain that men did not invent this system.

If it were up to men, all women would be equipped with special hormonal monitors to tell men such vital information as when it's a cry-free time of the month and when arousal is highest. Then we'd know when it's a good time for courting and when it's a better idea to run some errands. This would be a huge time-saver for everyone, but obviously nobody consulted men about how courtship should work.

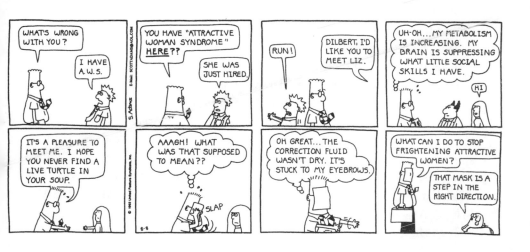

Fun

Nothing annoys women more than watching men have fun when there are heavy items in need of being moved to other places. If men ruled the world, all of those heavy objects would be in the right place to begin with, no matter where they were. But they aren't. Oh, no, everything is in the wrong place and must be moved now, not after your favorite television show is over.

Money

On average, men get paid more money than women. Most people think that is unfair, but let's look at it another way. Given a choice, most people would rather spend money than earn money. And who is doing all the spending?

If you don't believe that women spend most of the money, just walk into any Sears store and see what they're selling. If you're a male, you see maybe two things you might want—a second cordless drill (so you have a spare in the car) and a trickle charger, because you like how they look in the garage. That's all you want in the whole store. But SOMEONE is buying all that other stuff in there or Sears wouldn't be in business. Someone is buying those fuzzy toilet seat covers. Someone is buying decorative covers for tissue boxes. Someone is buying place mats.

Who could it be?

Kids don't have money. Pets aren't allowed in Sears. By the process of elimination, we can conclude that women must be buying all that other stuff. Women are spending most of the money.

If you were from another planet, such as Switzerland, and you only knew these two facts—1) Men earn most of the money, and 2) Women spend most of the money—what would you assume about who is holding whom by the whatchamacallits and swinging the person who owns the whatchamacallits around in the air while yelling, "I AM WOMAN, HEAR ME ROAR!"?

It's a rhetorical question.

Fashion

If men controlled fashion, they'd convince women to wear uncomfortable, pointy-heeled shoes that made legs look attractive. They'd promote bras that lifted the breasts upward for no apparent reason. The standard business attire for women would be skirts that display lots of leg. Men, on the other hand, would be able to get away with wearing a dull gray suit or jeans every single day.

Actually, I guess that's the way it is. Obviously, men control fashion. But that's the only thing men control.

In the short term, I predict women will try to tighten their grip on the world. We'll have more knickknacks and doilies than at any time in history. But that's in the near term. In the long term, technology will provide freedom for men, as I'll explain in the next section.

TECHNOLOGY TO FREE MEN

Scientists, most of them men, will continue to develop technologies that can provide men with freedom from the women who control every aspect of their lives except fashion.

PREDICTION 30

Most scientific and technical breakthroughs in the next century will be created by men and directed at finding replacements for women.

If you're looking to invest in the future, put your money in those areas that hold the most promise for replicating the roles of women:

- Genetic engineering.

- Virtual reality.

- Artificial intelligence.

- Internet.

- Robotics.

- Voice mail.

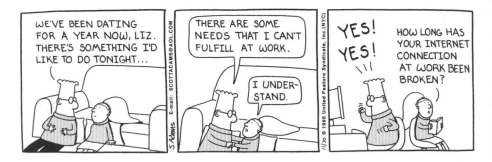

Those technologies that hold no promise as female replacements will stagnate. A good example of dead-end technology is air travel. It's essentially the same as it was thirty years ago—same cramped seats, same peanuts. The headphone technology has advanced all the way to "the hollow plastic tube." I'm not sure how ancient the flight control radar is, but I think it involves interns standing on top of the flight tower yelling, "Turn right! Turn right!" (More on this topic later.)

In contrast, during this extended period of airline technology stagnation, the nation's phone system has developed substantially. Your telephone has turned into a ubiquitous female presence through the widespread use of voice mail and audiotex systems that feature primarily feminine voices.

The "official" reason given for using female voices is that they are easier to hear, but I think it's obvious that the male technologists who promoted this technology wanted to have something on their desks that would sound like a woman and ask to be touched.

"Press one if you'd like to leave a message. Press two if it's the only action you'll get this month."

I THINK YOU LIKE THAT COMPUTER MORE THAN YOU LIKE ME.
S. Adams E-mail: SCOTTADAMS@AOL.COM
THAT'S NOT TRUE, LIZ. I DO NOT LIKE THAT COMPUTER MORE THAN I LIKE YOU.
7/12 © 1995 United Feature Syndicate, Inc. (NYC)
PLEASE, PLEASE DON'T ASK ABOUT THE LAPTOP.
"THAT" COMPUTER?

THE FUTURE OF WORK

THE FUTURE OF MANAGERS

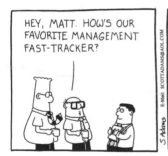
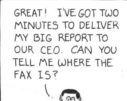
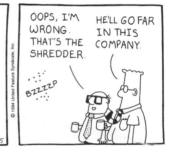

In an earlier book, *The Dilbert Principle*, I explained why incompetent employees are systematically identified and promoted to management. I will reiterate it here, in case you didn't read my earlier book, or you were drunk, or you refuse to listen, or you are not very bright, or you enjoy reading the same stuff twice. Your reasons are your own. I'm just trying to meet you halfway.

The underlying fact that prompted me to write *The Dilbert Principle* is that it takes less brains to be a manager than to be the people who are managed. For example, it takes a big ol' brain to write a computer program with a revolutionary new data encryption algorithm. A much smaller brain is needed to command that programmer to write status reports justifying his value.

If you're a surgeon, it takes a great deal of skill and intelligence to perform an organ transplant. It is much less challenging to write a mission statement for the hospital that explains your deep desire to avoid killing patients accidentally.

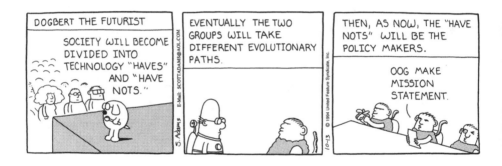

Middle management is becoming a dumping ground for professionals who have no special skills. It's the safest place to put them. You don't want one of them performing heart bypass surgery on you. There are already millions of highly skilled employees being managed by people who aren't nearly as bright, and this is not a stable situation.

Alleged True Story

The CEO of a small company decided they needed a motto to commemorate their longevity in the industry. This is what he came up with:

"Our innovation makes us first—our quality makes us last!"

The predictable result of the Dilbert Principle is that skilled professionals won't put up with the indignity of being "managed" by idiots.

PREDICTION 31

In the future, skilled professionals will flee their corporate jobs
and become their own bosses in ever-increasing numbers.
They'll become entrepreneurs, consultants, contractors, prostitutes,
and cartoonists.

Recently, an executive of a well-known magazine told me that he couldn't find any writers who were willing to join the company as employees. Several good writers were willing to work on a contractual basis, but none of them wanted a boss and a cubicle. Nor would they fall for the trick of agreeing to an exclusive contract. I predict you'll see a lot more of this in the future— the smartest professionals will avoid becoming either managers or employees. They'll have clients instead of bosses. They will be blissfully independent.

True Story

Yesterday at the airport I ran into an ex-coworker from my days at Pacific Bell. She quit the cubicle world two years ago to start her own consulting business. This week she hired her seventy-fifth employee.

We didn't have time to talk, because she was rushing off to exercise with her personal trainer.

The gutsiest professionals are already quitting their jobs and going it alone, but they're the exception. Most professionals are like sheep. (That's why so many business suits are made of wool, in case you wondered.) Employees have been conditioned by their employers to be timid and frightened. The sheepish employees will have to make the transition the way I did—by launching a new career from the security of a cubicle while still wearing a little wool outfit.

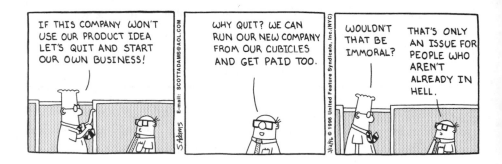

People often ask me how they can put energy into building a second career when they are already giving 100 percent to their current one. This would be a big problem if your salary and job security were somehow related to your performance. But that's living in the past. In the future, financial security will come primarily from your ability to divert company resources toward your new start-up business. I call it "employer financing." That way it doesn't sound so much like stealing. This is similar to when your boss refers to mandatory unpaid overtime as "being competitive."

Some people would say employer financing is unethical, maybe even illegal. That viewpoint is important to remember, because you'll want to remind people what they said later when they come to your new company and ask for a job.

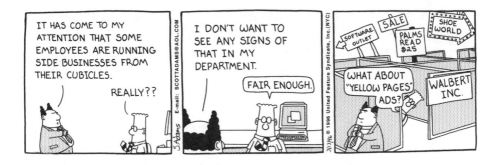

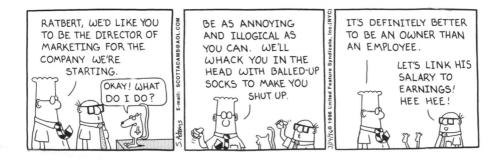

EMPLOYEE MOTIVATION

The current method of motivating employees involves frightening them until their arteries harden, then trying to make it all better by giving them inexpensive gifts bearing the company logo. Employees routinely trade their health for T-shirts, movie tickets, and framed certificates of accomplishments. To an objective observer—i.e., someone who doesn't care about you (i.e., your boss)—it would seem that employees are not very bright. But it wasn't always like this.

There was a time, years ago, when companies rewarded employees with a thing called "money." But after the "Dawn of Downsizing," the balance of power shifted completely to the employer. Companies didn't have to give away their hard-earned money to retain employees. They had too many workers already. What were the disgruntled employees going to do, quit?

This was a problem for middle managers. They were being paid to motivate the employees, but they didn't have the two tools that had always been effective in the past—money and the promise of job security. Managers needed new ways to dupe employees into working harder— ways that didn't cost anything.

With the help of highly paid consultants (i.e., people who had already been downsized), the managers hatched a wide range of "recognition" schemes that involved giving away things that come out of a laser printer instead of the U.S. Treasury.

This e-mail message describes one person's experience with a recognition award.

Subject: ataboys
From: (anonymous)
To: scottadams@aol.com

I just received an "ataboy" in the form of a time-off award. The letter I received described the events leading to the award and then it had this paragraph:

The above contributions resulted in a nonmeasurable benefit of small value and limited application. Therefore, four hours time off will be awarded to the employee.

Some "ataboy," eh?

Employees responded to the new recognition systems by staying at work for longer hours than ever. Most of that extra time was spent writing résumés and making long-distance calls from the fax room. But managers observed the employees staying in the office for longer hours and declared the recognition programs to be brilliant substitutes for money.

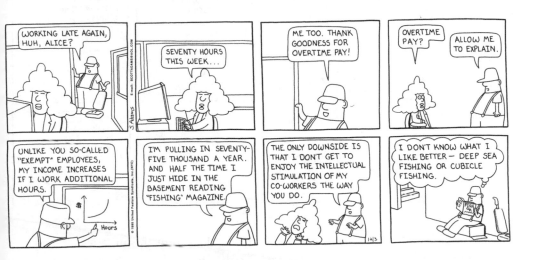

Somewhere right now I'm sure there is a manager sticking a bent paper clip into an eraser and wondering if he can pass it off as the "Excalibur Award for Excellence." He's thinking to himself that it's the recognition that counts, not the value of the gift. Any employee would be delighted to be recognized as a person who works eighty hours per week in return for a bent paper clip stuck in an eraser. That's exactly the kind of recognition employees crave—recognition as suckers.

Employees who don't appreciate "recognition" programs don't want to complain, because another downsizing could be around the corner.

Complaining during downsizing is like playing with a pogo stick in a fox-hole. It feels good, but it doesn't last.

THE REVENGE OF THE DOWNSIZED

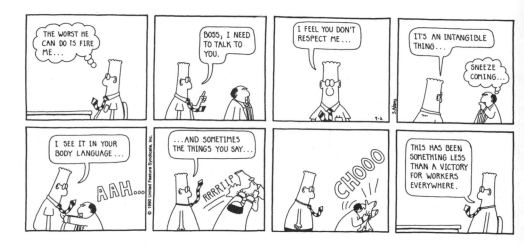

Working for a big company was a great deal until the nineties. If you could get hired, it was practically impossible to get fired. The biggest risk was that you'd cram too many office supplies in your pants and blow out a pocket.

Then the era of downsizing came. Employees were shoveled out the door faster than a pile of dead chipmunks at a cotillion. (And that's pretty darned fast even if I don't know what it means.) But many of the down-sizees had been avoiding real work by taking company-sponsored training courses for years. They were capable of doing excellent work if anybody had thought to ask. Suddenly, they were unemployed. Out of necessity, they reinvented themselves as "self-employed" people and scrambled to create new careers that would use the skills they learned while avoiding work.

Time passed. Then a funny thing happened. Downsized companies dis-covered they couldn't run a multinational company with just a CEO and a

Diversity Director. They needed employees. But it was too late to get their old employees back on the same basis. Companies couldn't offer job security without laughing. All they had was money. The balance of power had shifted. It became a seller's market for the most highly skilled workers.

PREDICTION 32

In the future, the balance of employment power will change.
We'll witness the revenge of the downsized.

It's not unusual to find companies where one-third of the technical staff are consultants and contract employees, some earning over $100 per hour. Unemployment pays very well if you do it right. Now everyone wants to get in the act.

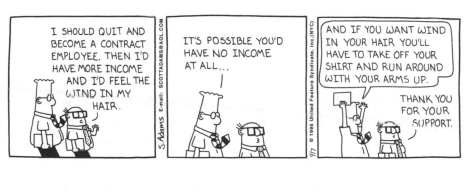

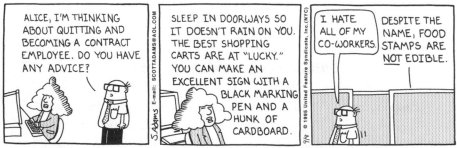

More people are discovering the joys of self-employment every year. Before long, they'll band together to get discounts on insurance, office equipment, training, and travel. They'll have their own magazines and conventions. They'll share information and blackball certain employers, cutting them off from the top talent. The self-employed will have power. Then the real fun begins.

The old-fashioned "job interview" will be a relic. Instead of the employer tormenting the helpless wannabe employee, you'll have the contract employees interviewing the employer.

Old Job Interview Process

Employer: I see that your name is Carl, but I'll call you pimple boy. Is that okay with you?

Job Seeker: Yes sir. You are very observant.

Employer: What is your biggest weakness, aside from your appearance, your lack of education, and your irrelevant experience?

Job Seeker: When I tongue-washed your car this morning, I forgot to move the car one foot ahead so I could wash the part of the tire that was on the ground.

Employer: INCOMPETENT FOOL! GET OUT OF MY OFFICE!

Future Job Interview Process

Employer: What can I do to convince you to accept obscene amounts of money to work here on a short-term contract basis? I'm begging. Please.

Contractor:	Well . . . I always wanted to have a pony.
Employer:	I'll get you a pony!
Contractor:	No, I want you to *be* my pony.

PREDICTION 33

In the future, highly qualified people will go on job interviews purely for recreation.

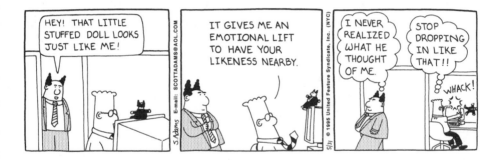

This new balance of power will be loads of fun for the contract employees, especially the bitter ones who were downsized. But despite the fun of being a contract employee, there will still be lots of regular employees. Their balance of power will also change, but in a totally different way. That leads me to the next topic.

THE JOB SEARCH IN THE FUTURE

Most people end up in their jobs by luck. For every person who planned a career, there are twenty who have stories that sound a lot like this one that I just made up:

Not a True Story

Well, one day I was riding my bike and a huge dog bit me and left me for dead. On the way to the hospital, a tanker truck ran a red light and collided with my ambulance, creating a gigantic explosion that propelled me across the street and onto a table at a sidewalk cafe. I started screaming, "WAA-OOO-AAHHH!" One of the patrons at the cafe was a music producer. IIe signed me to a five-record deal and drove me to the hospital. That's where I met my drummer.

Most people won't admit how they got their current jobs unless you push them up against a built-in wall unit and punch them in the stomach until they spill their drink and start yelling, "I'LL NEVER INVITE YOU TO ONE OF MY PARTIES AGAIN, YOU DRUNKEN FOOL!" I think the reason these annoying people won't tell me how they got their jobs is because they are embarrassed to admit luck was involved. I can't blame them. Typically, the pre-luck part of their careers involved doing something enormously pathetic.

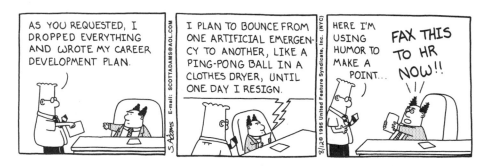

Take me, for example. I'm a successful cartoonist and author because I'm a complete failure at being an employee of the local phone company. Despite the fact that my co-workers were so lifeless they were often mistaken for mannequins, I was not streaking past them on my way up the career ladder. I didn't have the hair or height to succeed in management. Instead, I spent my time mocking successful managers and accidentally preparing for my future career.

I learned to draw when I was a kid because the alternative forms of entertainment were limited. I didn't grow up in what you'd call "a town with intellectually stimulating people." I suppose I could have made friends with the kids my age who were fascinated with the interaction of firecrackers and frogs, but science didn't interest me at the time.

We had a television, but we only received one channel clearly. It required some ingenuity to do any channel surfing, especially since we didn't have a remote control. I would wait until my little sister wandered by and then yell, "Cindy, change the channel while you're up." This was very funny until the millionth time, after which she broke my jaw with a hassock.

My only other choices for entertainment were drawing cartoons or playing Scrabble with Mom. Mom took her Scrabble very seriously. She was a brutal competitor. In fact, she didn't teach me any language skills until I reached the age of six, because she figured that would give her an edge in Scrabble later on. I was in college before I figured out that Webster didn't really make any last-minute handwritten additions to the dictionary. To this day I still wonder about her claim that head-butting is allowed in Scrabble.

So I ended up drawing cartoons alone in my room because it didn't require any language skills and I wouldn't have to watch my Mom do that damned victory dance on the kitchen table. If I wrote a completely accurate résumé for myself right now, I'd have to say something like, "Leveraged my inadequacies into a career that involves making fun of people who are more successful in business than I am."

There are some exceptions to the career luck rule. For example, lawyers and doctors study for years to prepare for their professions, diligently acquiring valuable information that they can use later in lieu of personalities. But the rest of us don't have a clear career path. If we're lucky, we're bitten by large dogs and propelled into sidewalk cafes where something lucky happens.

It's a good thing that career luck happens so often. It's more effective than the alternative—lying on your résumé and hoping you get an interview with someone who has poor perception.

The current job-filling process has been a wonderful thing for unqualified people. I was a major beneficiary of the system in my corporate past. I could always count on moving to a new job within the company, assisted by the fact that the hiring manager didn't have a good system for finding a better candidate. My employer's lack of alternatives was my gain.

But what happens when every job opening and every résumé is on the Internet? Surely that will happen. You'll suddenly find yourself competing against *thousands* of candidates for every low- and medium-skill job. You won't be able to rely on the inefficiency of the job search process anymore.

Companies will be able to find a candidate who not only fits a job perfectly without training, but might be willing to do it for *less* than the normal salary for that position. For example, someone in a godforsaken hellhole like North Dakota might want to move to California and be willing to accept a low salary to do it. In fact, they might be willing to do it without demanding that their relocation costs be paid. In fact, they might be willing to strap their livestock to their backs and walk to California. (Note: If you are a resident of the godforsaken hellhole of North Dakota, the only thing I actually know about your state is that you don't buy many *Dilbert* books. The conclusion that it is a hellhole follows logically. If this bothers you, I suggest that you move to South Dakota where you can get some respect.)

For the first time in history, companies will have an abundance of good applicants for every job opening in the "medium-skill" level. That means salaries for medium-skilled jobs will go down, unless the government gets involved. If the government notices what's happening to salaries, they will step in and do what governments always do for the powerless—they'll raise their taxes. So it's bad news all around.

PREDICTION 34

In the future, salaries will go down for people in medium-skilled
jobs, thanks to the godforsaken hellhole called North Dakota.

It's happy days ahead for the highly skilled laborer. The job market will start to look like the NBA. Top technical people will command amazingly obscene salaries. The employee who is 1 percent better in a high-skill area is worth a hundred times as much as someone who is just "pretty good." That 1 percent might be the difference between winning and losing in the marketplace—just as it is in sports.

Professional sports is a good model for how the rest of the economy will look in the future. Pro sports is an industry where there is almost complete information about who has what skills and who has what openings. It's a fairly efficient job market.

In the NBA, you end up with amazingly rich athletes on one end of the scale and everyone else who works for the club has job descriptions like, "Guy who wipes perspiration off the court during time-outs." There are a few executives in the middle to hold it all together, but they aren't terribly important.

That's what the job market will look like in the future—rich superstar professionals on one end of the spectrum, perspiration wipers on the other, and a few managers in the middle. Everything else will be done by consultants or outsourcing firms.

PREDICTION 35

In the future, employees will either be superstars or perspiration
wipers. Those who aren't qualified to do either will become managers.

OUTSOURCING

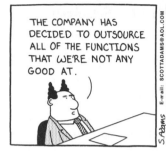
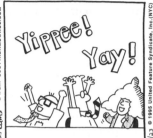
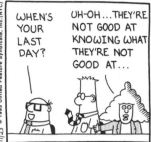

My mother always told me to beware of strangers. But over time, I've noticed that strangers are consistently nicer than the people I know. I don't think it's a coincidence. I have to conclude that all of the insightful, talented, and generous people in the world are in fact strangers.

Many companies have reached the same conclusion. They know that it's a waste of time to have their own bumbling employees perform important functions. It's better to trust those functions to the people who have our best interests in mind (i.e., complete strangers in distant lands). This is the concept behind "outsourcing," and it's a good one.

I use outsourcing in my job, too. My cats were my in-house legal department until I discovered they were coughing up hairballs and recording the time as billable hours. Now I pay a human being in another city to handle my legal stuff. He still coughs up hairballs, but he has the professional courtesy to call it "phone conversation" when he lists it on the invoice.

When you're trying to outsource work, always select the low-cost provider. Quality isn't important, because you can always fix that later by learning the native tongue of your supplier and making threatening phone calls in the middle of the night. The only risk is that the electrical impulses from your telephone network won't travel across the baling twine used as a phone network in your supplier's country. Sometimes you can compensate by yelling.

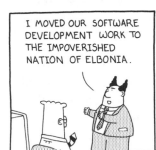
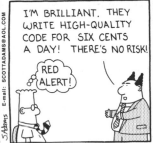
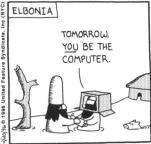

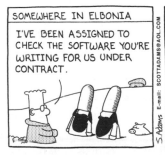
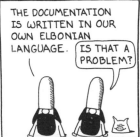
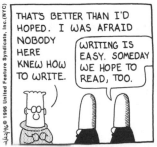

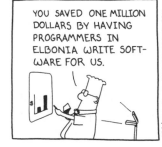
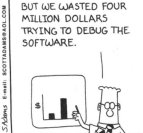
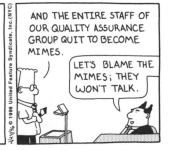

PREDICTION 36

In the future, all work will be outsourced, until all the work on the
planet is being done by one guy.

In the future, all companies will outsource their work to other companies who will subcontract their work to yet other companies. Eventually,
there will be one guy doing all the work on Earth. This will all be well and
good until one day he calls in sick and the entire economy of the planet is
plunged into a depression. Until that happens, there's no real downside.

If you want to thrive in an era of outsourcing, try to avoid being that one
guy who does everyone's work. He'll make a lot of money in the short run,
but you know he's going to take the blame when things go terribly wrong.

THE JOB MODEL OF THE FUTURE

I'm convinced that my job situation is a model of the future. This chapter
is being written as I sit alone in my home office in my pajamas. (They're
red flannel, just so you can picture it.) The only noise is the whir of my
hard disk and the sound of my cat, Sarah, chewing through my modem
cables.

I have no employees at the moment, yet the *Dilbert* business is generating record sales and reaching 140 million readers every day. My relationship with the hundreds of professionals who bring *Dilbert* to the market is
contractual. I am blissful in my non-boss environment.

I've noticed that when people have contracts, they do what the contract
says. Full-time employees have fuzzier objectives. They often feel under-
paid and abused. They don't have much incentive to do the right thing,
especially since big raises and promotions are mostly history.

In those rare situations where employees have clear objectives and good
intentions, their efforts are blocked by various mandatory productivity-
thwarting activities:

Productivity-Thwarting Activities

- Mandatory dress code.

- Mandatory safety training.

- Mandatory sexual harassment training.

- Mandatory diversity training.

- Mandatory United Way kick-off meeting.

- Mandatory staff meetings.

When you work alone, everything is optional, including clothes. I can do dangerous things if I want to. I can do dangerous things naked if I want to. I can sexually harass myself while doing dangerous things naked. And I can insult myself for doing it. Best yet, I can do it during the time I've scheduled for my own staff meeting. I try to do all of those things as often as possible.

If you're an employee of a big company, you've probably spent hours contributing to the creation of your department's mission statement. I also have a mission statement, but I didn't have to consider the inane opinions of any co-workers when I wrote it. My entire mission statement took twelve seconds to write. It goes like this:

Scott Adams's Mission Statement

"Rub my bald spot once a day."

My mission statement doesn't help me make more money. It doesn't even make sense. But I've never seen a mission statement that met either of those tests. At least I didn't spend much time writing mine. That's more than you can say if you work for a big company.

Here is a selection of cartoons that best describe the productivity and effectiveness of the typical office environment. If you haven't already decided to work for yourself, this should push you over the edge.

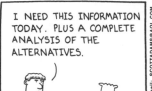

I NEED THIS INFORMATION TODAY. PLUS A COMPLETE ANALYSIS OF THE ALTERNATIVES.

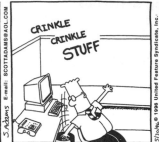

CRINKLE
CRINKLE
STUFF

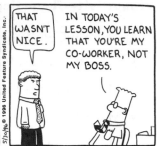

THAT WASN'T NICE.

IN TODAY'S LESSON, YOU LEARN THAT YOU'RE MY CO-WORKER, NOT MY BOSS.

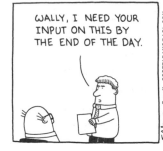

WALLY, I NEED YOUR INPUT ON THIS BY THE END OF THE DAY.

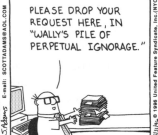

PLEASE DROP YOUR REQUEST HERE, IN "WALLY'S PILE OF PERPETUAL IGNORAGE."

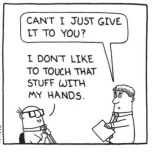

CAN'T I JUST GIVE IT TO YOU?

I DON'T LIKE TO TOUCH THAT STUFF WITH MY HANDS.

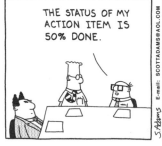

THE STATUS OF MY ACTION ITEM IS 50% DONE.

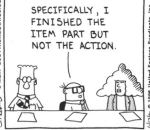

SPECIFICALLY, I FINISHED THE ITEM PART BUT NOT THE ACTION.

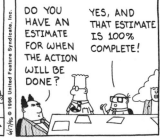

DO YOU HAVE AN ESTIMATE FOR WHEN THE ACTION WILL BE DONE?

YES, AND THAT ESTIMATE IS 100% COMPLETE!

I COULD SIT HERE DOING NOTHING.
OR I COULD IMPLEMENT A BOLD QUALITY INITIATIVE WITH THE HELP OF MY TALENTED AND ENERGETIC CO-WORKERS.
I CRACK ME UP.
www.unitedmedia.com
6/25/96 © 1996 United Feature Syndicate, Inc.(NYC)

AND TED GETS THIS "SINGULAR ACHIEVEMENT" AWARD FOR CREATING THE "WE ARE TEAMS" CAMPAIGN.
IT'S A CHECK FOR A THOUSAND DOLLARS! LET'S ALL GIVE TED A HAND.
SLAP
WHACK
OW!!
THESE THINGS NEVER WORK THE WAY YOU WANT THEM TO.
E-mail: SCOTTADAMS@AOL.COM
© 1995 United Feature Syndicate, Inc. (NYC)
2/28

I'D LIKE TO KICK-OFF THE PROJECT WITH THE TRADITIONAL BAD-MOUTHING OF THE GUY WHO WORKED ON THIS BEFORE.
HE'S SO SLIMY THAT SLUGS POUR SALT ON HIM. HIS BRAIN WOULD RATTLE IN A FLEA'S SKULL!
OH, AND I'LL NEED YOUR FILES.
FLEAS DON'T HAVE "SKULLS"!!
E-mail: SCOTTADAMS@AOL.COM
3-3 © 1995 United Feature Syndicate, Inc. (NYC)

I'M WRITING AN E-MAIL TO PROTEST THE NEW POLICY OF MAKING THE EMPLOYEES EMPTY THEIR OWN TRASH AT NIGHT.

IT'S STUPID TO HAVE HIGHLY PAID ENGINEERS DOING UNPRODUCTIVE TASKS WHEN WE COULD BE INVENTING THE FUTURE!

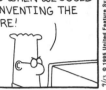

ARE YOU COMING TO THE "QUALITY FAIRE"?

NO, THIS WILL TAKE ANOTHER HOUR.

WHERE ARE YOU TAKING ALL OF THAT OFFICE EQUIPMENT?

I'M HAVING A GARAGE SALE.

OUR NEW COMPANY SLOGAN IS "ACT LIKE YOU OWN THE COMPANY." SO I'VE BEEN SELLING THE STUFF THAT I DON'T USE AND KEEPING THE MONEY.

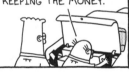

IS THAT MY NEW COLOR MONITOR?

YEAH, I NEVER USED THAT THING.

I'M HAPPY TO REPORT THAT I HAVE EMBRACED THE NEW COMPANY SLOGAN "ACT LIKE YOU OWN THE COMPANY."

THIS MORNING I FIRED THE MARKETING DEPARTMENT AND HAD SECURITY ESCORT THEM OUT.

THAT'S NOT EXACTLY WHAT WE HAD IN MIND...

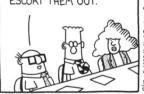

FORTUNATELY I ANTICIPATED YOUR REACTION.

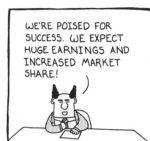

WE'RE POISED FOR SUCCESS. WE EXPECT HUGE EARNINGS AND INCREASED MARKET SHARE!

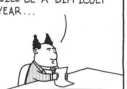

NEXT ON THE AGENDA... THERE WILL BE NO RAISES BECAUSE IT WILL BE A DIFFICULT YEAR...

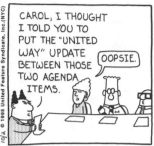

CAROL, I THOUGHT I TOLD YOU TO PUT THE "UNITED WAY" UPDATE BETWEEN THOSE TWO AGENDA ITEMS.

OOPSIE.

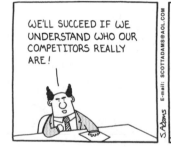

WE'LL SUCCEED IF WE UNDERSTAND WHO OUR COMPETITORS REALLY ARE!

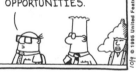

MY COMPETITION IS DILBERT AND ALICE, WITH WHOM I COMPETE FOR SALARY INCREASES AND RARE PROMOTION OPPORTUNITIES.

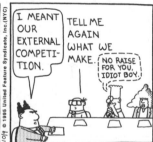

I MEANT OUR EXTERNAL COMPETITION.

TELL ME AGAIN WHAT WE MAKE.

NO RAISE FOR YOU, IDIOT BOY.

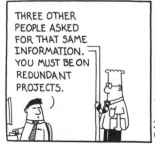

THREE OTHER PEOPLE ASKED FOR THAT SAME INFORMATION. YOU MUST BE ON REDUNDANT PROJECTS.

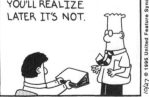

HERE'S A BIG BINDER WHICH AT FIRST GLANCE SEEMS USEFUL, BUT YOU'LL REALIZE LATER IT'S NOT.

I'VE GOT A FEW MORE USELESS BINDERS. DO YOU WANT 'EM?

SURE. I'M USING THEM TO BUILD AN ADDITION TO MY CUBICLE.

I DON'T MIND DONATING BLOOD... IT'S GOOD FOR SOCIETY...
FORM LINE
E-Mail: SCOTTADAMS@AOL.COM
S. Adams
BUT I'M WORRIED THAT OUR COMPANY IS GETTING TOO COMPETITIVE ABOUT HOW MUCH WE GIVE COMPARED TO OTHER COMPANIES.
© 1994 United Feature Syndicate, Inc.
11-8
MAN, I'M THIRSTY!!

I JUST LOST THE SUBTLE MENTAL CONNECTION BETWEEN MY PERFORMANCE AND MY SALARY.
E-Mail: SCOTTADAMS@AOL.COM
S. Adams
I GET PAID THE SAME NO MATTER WHAT I DO. I CAN STAND HERE AND FLICK MY FINGERS AND STILL GET PAID.
FLICK FLICK FLICK
11-23
© 1994 United Feature Syndicate, Inc.
DO YOU REALIZE WHAT THIS MEANS??!
FLICK FLICK
HEY! YOU'RE GETTING PAID FOR THAT!

MY ACCOMPLISHMENT THIS WEEK IS THAT I'VE BECOME AN AGENT OF CHANGE.
S. Adams E-mail: SCOTTADAMS@AOL.COM
I FOSTER AND REWARD THOSE BEHAVIORS THAT CONTRIBUTE TO A CULTURE OF TEAMWORK.
11/15 © 1995 United Feature Syndicate, Inc.(NYC)
I'VE BECOME SLIGHTLY MORE CYNICAL.
KEEP UP THE GOOD WORK, BUDDY.
PAT PAT

PREDICTION 37

In the future, more people will work for themselves, creating a huge market for bizarre products.

Obviously, with a work environment like Dilbert's, a growing number of people will choose to work at home. There's a huge market opportunity for anyone who can figure out what products to sell to people who work at home. Three ideas come to mind:

Products Needed for the Work-at-Home Market

- Smell-o-meter to remind you when to bathe.

- Anti-cat guard for your computer keyboard.

- Pants with special holsters for holding bananas. (I like to snack during the day and I resent the trips to the kitchen.)

I also want a fake "call-waiting" feature for my phone. That would be a huge time-saver, because my friends think that just because I'm sitting around in my pajamas rubbing my bald spot, I'm not working. They don't know that is exactly what my mission statement says I should be doing. I'd like to be able to tell the people who call me, "Ooh, It sounds like I have another call. Would you mind hanging up and never calling again?" I already say that to people, but I think some are catching on that I'm making the call-waiting sound by whistling.

THE FUTURE OF TELECOMMUTING

A growing number of workers—those who are more clever than industrious—have already discovered the unbridled joy of sitting at home and getting paid for sleeping, eating, masturbating, and watching television. This technique—sometimes called telecommuting—has all the financial advantages of being employed with none of the stigma of being a filthy, perverted hobo.

PREDICTION 38

In the future, filthy, perverted hobos will refer to themselves as telecommuters, until someone points out that they aren't being paid.

Telecommuting is much better than the alternative of going into the office and having your co-workers peck you to death like a flock of chickens on a tissue-paper bag full of corn. (Please take a moment to savor that analogy. If you close your eyes, you can almost hear the chickens clucking.)

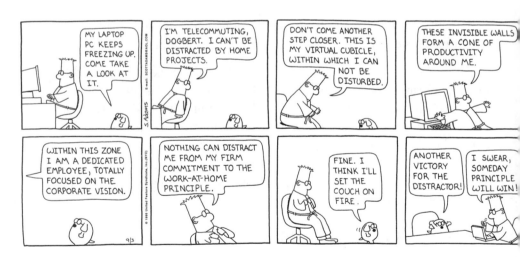

Those of you who are foolish enough to transport your bodies to the office are faced with the daily horror of what some people have begun calling "negative work."

NEGATIVE WORK FORMULA

Real Work + Negative Work = Zero Work

For example, let's say you need some vital information from a co-worker in order to do "real work." Your co-worker is likely to generate enough "negative work" to cancel your productivity for the day.

Example of Negative Work in Action

You: Please give me that vital information that you alone possess.

Co-worker: Sure, but while I've got you here, why don't you attend my project meeting?

You: Um . . . what does your project have to do with me?

Co-worker: It's an important project. You should be there to provide your valuable input.

You: I don't even know what your project is about.

Co-worker: Of course not! You haven't attended any of the meetings. It starts in ten minutes. I'll give you the vital information right afterward. Heck, we might even discuss the vital information during the meeting. You don't want to miss that, do you?

(At this point in the conversation, you realize you will never get help from this co-worker again unless you cave in to this ludicrous request.)

You: Well, okay, I guess.

Co-worker: Great. Oh, and bring a pad. It's your turn to
                      take the minutes.

The result of this is negative work.

Productivity in the modern office can be scored like golf, as in "I'm three under for the day." For every unit of work, there is at least one off-setting unit of negative work created by your Induhvidual co-workers.

It's worse for women, of course, because male Induhviduals know that flirting with female co-workers looks exactly like work. Males naturally want to talk to as many women as possible during the day. This maximizes their enjoyment and income while trading off nothing except shareholder value—and that belongs to people who should know better than to invest in your company. So it's hard to feel sorry for them.

The lonelier the guy and the more attractive the woman, the greater the amount of negative work that will be generated. For lonely guys, a business meeting with attractive co-workers is like a date, except at the end of the meeting, the women give you correct phone numbers. Speaking as a guy who has dated, this is a big improvement.

I realize it's unwise to go deeper into this topic during times of great sensitivity about diversity in the workplace, but there's something that all women need to know about men in order to understand what's behind much of the negative work. Here it is. The secret that all males in the workplace don't want women to know is:

WE'RE THINKING ABOUT HAVING SEX WITH YOU!

If you're a woman, you're thinking, "Duh." You already knew that. The part you probably don't know is *when* men think it and how often.

The "how often" part is whenever you're talking. Men can only do one thing at a time. We're notorious single-taskers. We can't speak a sentence and hold a good fantasy at the same time, so when *we're* talking, we're *not* fantasizing. But when a woman is talking to a man, the man has two choices:

1. Listen.

2. Fantasize about having sex with the woman who is generating all that noise.

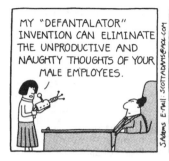 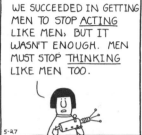 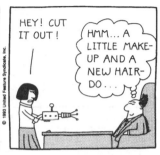

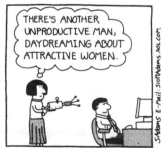 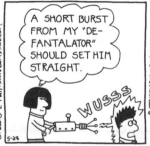 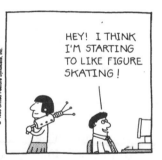

This explains the common complaint that women have about men—we don't listen. It's not because we don't *want* to listen to what you have to say, but that we can't do two things at once. Listening never gets higher than the number-two priority. (Okay, maybe that's the same as saying we don't *want* to listen. But let's not get all caught up in semantics.)

The reason I can safely reveal this secret is that men already know it and women won't believe it. Women are multitaskers. I'll bet women can mix a fantasy with their conversation without missing a beat. Women probably think men are like that, too—capable of entertaining mild fantasies throughout the day without losing focus or drifting in and out of comas. Well, we can't. When you're talking, we're thinking intensely about having sex with you. If you're unattractive, we're focusing on the woman just over your shoulder. It's not something we're proud of. It's just the way we're wired.

If there are any women who think I'm overgeneralizing, I'll be happy to meet with you to listen to your point of view. But please bring a cute friend as an emergency backup in case you're wrong.

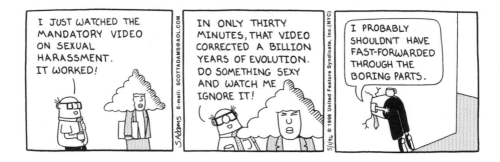

Telecommuting isn't for everyone. It takes a certain kind of person to be able to work alone. I recommend trying telecommuting for one week and then taking this quiz to see if you have what it takes to enjoy it.

Telecommuting Enjoyment Test

- Did you at any time open the refrigerator and start shoveling anything that wasn't stuck to the shelf toward the big hole in your face?

- Did you at any time take a conference call in the nude and experience an intense guilty pleasure?

- Did you at any time curse at an inanimate object and later apologize to it?

- Did you at any time engage in solo sex and yell out, "I'M GETTING PAID FOR THIS! HA HA HA HA HA!"?

If you said yes to any of those questions, you should be telecommuting more often.

THE FUTURE OF OFFICE WORKSTATIONS

When I first joined the work force in 1979, anybody with a body temperature over eighty degrees qualified for a private office with a door. Those were glorious, carefree days. I was working for a huge California bank. Every day, I would close the door to my private office and spend hours making personal phone calls, balancing my checkbook, and flirting with attractive female co-workers. Sometimes I flirted with unattractive female co-workers, but in my defense, I considered it "practice."

Thousands of my co-workers were doing similar things behind their own closed doors, except for the handful of attractive co-workers who were forced to roam from office to office to keep the system working.

Eventually, my company was purchased by its competitor for the price of $12 plus some postage stamps (I forget the exact figure), and most of my co-workers were fired. I escaped their fate by calling upon my most valuable professional resource—luck—which allowed me to attach myself in a barnacle-like fashion to another big company in the nick of time. I even got a large undeserved salary increase too.

Although I successfully leveraged my incompetence into a better job, I still looked back with bitterness, dismay, and yes, sometimes laughter. The laughter part was usually when my ex–co-workers called to ask if there were any openings at my company. I found 100 different ways to tell them that my new company had much higher standards, and it wasn't really an option they should be considering.

Although I was out of banking, I couldn't stop wondering what the victorious bank had that my old vanquished bank didn't have. Why could one company triumph where one had failed? In time, I uncovered their secret: cubicles.

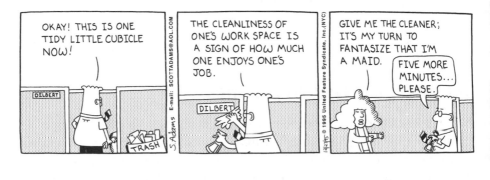

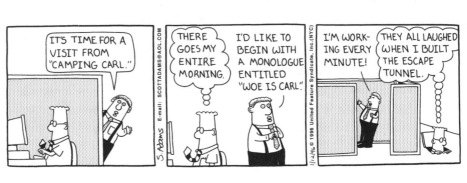

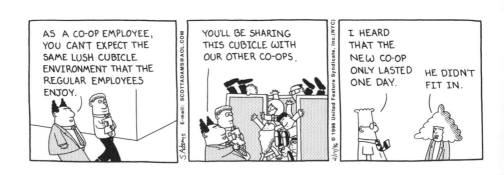

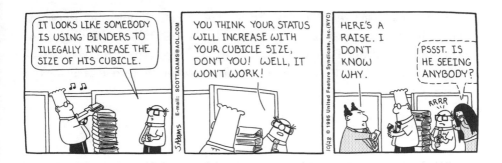

The bank discovered that when employees were taken out of private offices and put in tiny, fabric-covered containers, they became competitive dynamos. These cubicle-bound titans used less real estate, heating, and cooling. And the sleek, doorless design cut way back on the flirting and personal calls. Those workers became unstoppable, productive juggernauts capable of squashing any sissified office-dwelling company.

Employee communication increased significantly. With the open-cubicle design, they could hear not only the conversations directed at themselves, but also the conversations directed at anyone else. And they weren't limited to audio inputs. They could read the body language of everyone in the office who waddled past the cubicles all day long.

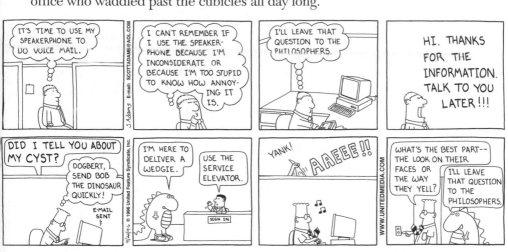

That bank hasn't rested on its laurels. They're still innovating. Recently, they improved the restrooms by removing all the stalls and adding windows to the hallway. Result: Nobody goes in there to read the sports section anymore. Profits have zoomed. It looks like another good year for the stockholders.

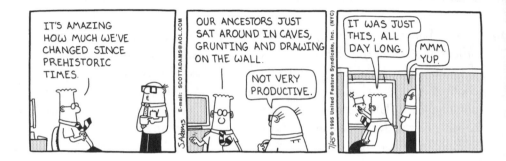

But what of the future of office workstations? Nothing ever stays the same. It's safe to predict that cubicles are not the ultimate answer for office space. So let's follow the logic and see where it leads.

Cubicles are more competitive than private offices, but they still have a lot of wasted room. A fully occupied cubicle is 70 percent air. That waste has not escaped the notice of workstation designers. Most of the unused airspace will be driven out of the design of future work areas. This is already happening at many companies, albeit gradually, as they replace larger cubicles with ever-smaller versions. This practice even has a name at some companies: "densification." But it won't end there.

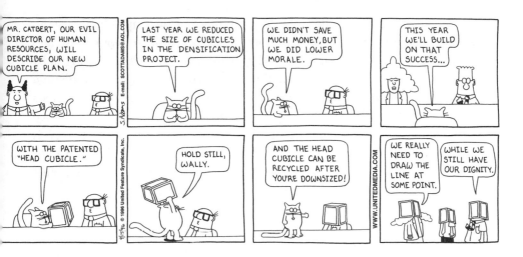

I see the workstation of the future looking like a high-tech hairdresser's chair. You'll have your computer built into the base of the chair and the keyboard swinging onto your lap from the side. No desk surface will be needed. An oversized helmet-like device (let's call it a "head cubicle") will be attached to the back of your chair and cover your head for privacy. On the inside of the head cubicle will be a display screen, speakers, and a microphone. Every unit will be wired to the Internet and the public phone system. These workstations will be lined up side by side in warehouse-like office spaces in dangerous neighborhoods. You'll be able to shout and sing and moan in your head cubicle without disturbing your co-worker who is two feet away. And you won't hear his annoying cries for help after sustaining a bullet wound on the way to work.

PREDICTION 39

In the future, aggressive companies will replace standard cubicles with head cubicles.

New technology will allow managers to monitor the unproductive activities of each employee as never before. Sensors will detect your pulse and breathing rates to determine whether you're downloading pornography from the Internet or doing anything else that is fun or stimulating. Monitors will detect REM patterns and beep whenever an employee nods off. Employees will learn to stay in a narrow range of joyless existence between happiness (which shouldn't be compensated) and sleep (which is unproductive). Let's call that the "Compensated Work Zone," or CWZ for short. I don't plan to use the phrase ever again for the rest of my life, but I think we can all admit we like acronyms and leave it at that.

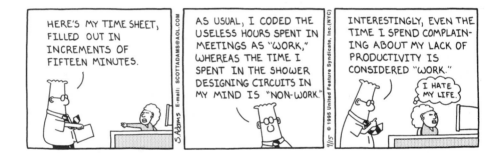

You won't need conference rooms, because everyone will be able to attend virtual meetings without leaving the chair. Visitors from the outside will get their own special chairs in the lobby so they never have to see the employees in person.

The virtual meetings won't use video conferencing technology in the way most people imagine. There's one huge drawback to video conferencing: Many employees are ugly. Logically, it is a waste of bandwidth to transmit an image of something you'd be better off not looking at. If you think about it, there are very few of your co-workers who have faces you'd like to see more often. I've never met anyone who kept pictures of their co-workers on their desk in little frames. It's rare to find anyone carrying a picture of a co-worker in their wallet. So then why on Earth would we want to transmit their ugly faces across the network and have them appear two feet from our noses?

The obvious solution—and inevitable by any reasoned opinion—is that people will send digitally enhanced images to represent themselves at meetings. This will solve the ugliness *and* the dress code problem at the same time.

Every employee will have a chance to create their own digital representative. There will be corporate guidelines of course, which I imagine will look something like this:

Corporate Guidelines for Digital Representatives (DR)

1. Your DR may not be a nudist.

2. Your DR may not resemble our CEO in leather chaps.

3. Your DR's head and buttocks must be clearly differentiated.

4. Your DR may not be visibly aroused.

ACRONYMS SHORTAGES

There are only twenty-six letters in the alphabet. Eventually, all of the good acronyms that are less than four letters will be used up. This will be a major problem for businesses.

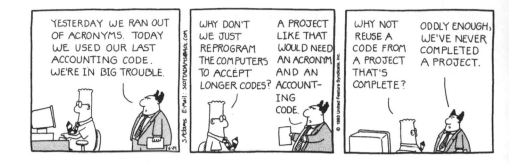

We'll also start running out of new company names and logo designs. The first sign of trouble—and we're already seeing it—is when major companies begin using coffee stains for logos.*

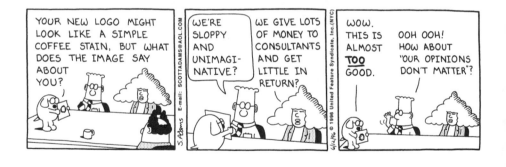

We're already starting to scrape the bottom of the name barrel.

*After the Brown Ring of Quality strips were published in the newspaper, I got many e-mail messages from people who assumed I was referring to AT&T's Lucent spin-off. Many other people wrote to say it reminded them of their own logos. Apparently, the coffee stain concept was a popular one.

PREDICTION 40

In the future, your only choices for new project names will be ones that sound undignified.

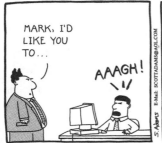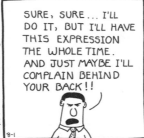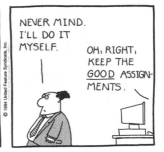

True Story

At one technology company, the senior management became angered that two important projects had been named Ren and Stimpy, after famous cartoon characters. They declared that henceforth there would be a master namer who would approve the names of all future projects. The master namer would choose from a list of famous river names to ensure appropriate and dignified names.

The process worked well until engineers presented the status of projects Ubangi and Volga. Senior management was livid until someone explained that those are the names of rivers.

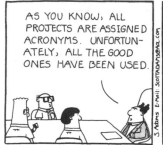 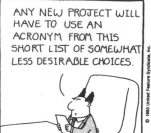 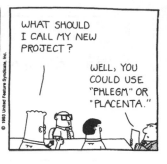

INDUSTRIAL ESPIONAGE

Industrial espionage sounds like a great concept on paper. The theory is that your competitors know something important that you should also know.

PREDICTION 41

In the future, it will become increasingly obvious that your competitors are just as clueless as you are.

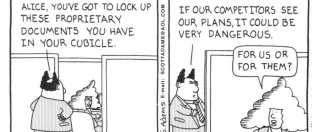 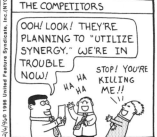

NINE

MARKETING IN THE FUTURE

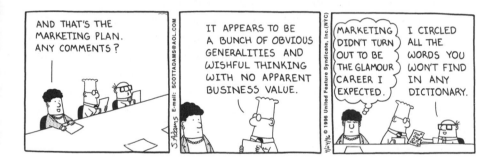

In the past, every successful company had some sort of "barrier to entry" that kept other companies from swooping in and stealing their customers.

PREDICTION 42

In the future, all barriers to entry will go away and companies will be forced to form what I call "confusopolies."

Confusopoly: A group of companies with similar products who intentionally confuse customers instead of competing on price.

All the things that used to be barriers to entry are disappearing, thanks to huge improvements in technology, capital markets, transportation, and communication. Any company can enter any other business by buying the parts they need and putting them together. You can buy the people, the knowledge, the equipment, and the market research. In theory, every company in the future will be able to figure out exactly what the customer wants and then buy the resources needed to produce it. Even patents are becoming less of a barrier, because there is always a way to engineer around them. Without exception, all the things that have been traditional barriers to entry are diminishing in importance.

A hundred years ago, it was only practical to have one major phone company serving the United States. Today, there are lots of choices and more on the way. They all provide nearly identical service. You would think this would create a price war and drive the prices down to the cost of providing it (that's what I learned between naps in my economics classes), but it isn't happening. The companies are forming efficient confusopolies so customers can't tell who has the lowest prices. Companies have learned to use the complexities of life as an economic tool.

A few short years ago, a tiny software startup called Netscape Communications built an Internet browser that threatened to dethrone Microsoft's stranglehold on computer software. Within a year, Microsoft was able to buy all the talent and resources it needed to build a similar product that didn't violate any patents or copyrights. That's the model of the future: Any new product can be rapidly matched by a determined competitor. Browser software is just complicated enough that I can't tell which one would be better for the things I might be doing in the future. Netscape and Microsoft have formed a confusopoly, thus guaranteeing that both will survive and prosper.

Several other industries are already dominated by confusopolies:

Existing Confusopolies

- Telephone service.

- Insurance.

- Mortgage loans.

- Banking.

- Financial services.

Those types of companies are natural confusopolies, because they offer products that would be indistinguishable to the customer except for the great care taken to make them intentionally confusing.

Companies form confusopolies to make it impossible for the average Induhvidual to determine who has the lowest price. This way each major company gets a share of the pie, the size of which depends on how skillfully they can dupe ignorant customers with advertisements. That will be the primary job of marketing professionals in the future—disguising the true cost of your product in order to be a successful confusopolist.

I recently had a conversation with a top executive for an energy company. He told me that in the near future I would be able to specify which company I wanted to provide electricity to my house. My local power utility will handle all of the physical connections and billing, but I will be able to specify which company actually produces the electricity I buy. Uh-oh.

This means—lord help us all—that power companies will soon form confusopolies and fill the advertising channels with information about the quality of their electricity. They will accuse the competitors of having defective electricity. Celebrities will be hired as electricity spokespersons. People will want to use the electricity that Michael Jordan uses, because it will be so much better.

You'll see magazine ads featuring toast made with the competitor's electricity, all spotty and burnt, compared to perfect toast made with the advertiser's electricity.

Eventually, word will get around that electricity is pretty much the same regardless of who makes it. So marketing will begin to focus on confusing people about the true price. Each power company will have different electricity pricing models that claim to be the cheapest.

Electricity Advertisements

- Only a dime per watt!

- Lease your electricity, don't buy!

- Huge discounts on off-peak usage!

- Big savings for frequent microwavers!

The vast array of confusing choices will anger you as a consumer, but you will have to pick one—unless you crave the Unabomber lifestyle (which looks more rational every day). You'll choose your power company by using sophisticated analytical methods, such as looking at the names of each company and trying to decide which one sounds like they have "good people."

In a future where confusion is the most important competitive asset, the successful companies are the ones who do it best. Dogbert would make an excellent entrepreneur in that environment.

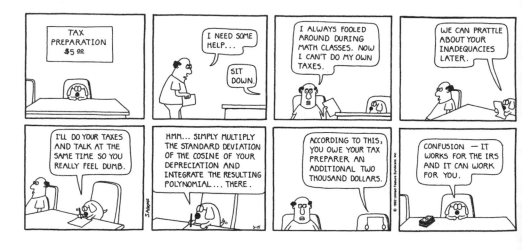

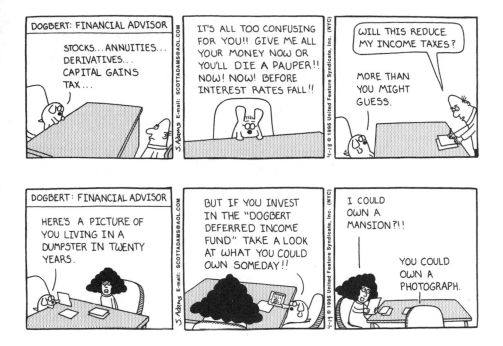

In the future, if all products and services are essentially the same, only the effectiveness of advertisements will set them apart.

PREDICTION 43

In the future, the science of advertising will improve to the point where buying what you see in an advertisement is no longer optional.

Every human skill improves over time. Athletes are faster and stronger every year. Medicine saves more lives. Teachers learn better teaching techniques. Logically, advertising skills will also continue to improve.

Hundreds of years ago, advertisements were created to generate awareness. Then they improved to the point of being persuasive. Now they're
downright manipulative. The next step—and we're almost there—is where
advertisements are so effective that you will be compelled to buy whatever
they tell you to buy.

The only choices you'll be able to make is where you choose to see the
advertisements. If you tune your radio to KFOG, you end up buying a
Ford. If you tune your radio to K101, you buy a Honda. Your purchasing
decisions will be limited to your choice of radio stations. The radio spon-
sors will decide what car you buy. When you run out of money, you'll close
the blinds, turn off the electricity to your house, and wait for the next paycheck to arrive. Your only defense will be to hide from the ads.

Everyone has a weak spot when it comes to advertisements. For example, I'll buy anything that Cindy Crawford is selling. I have a garage full of
Revlon products, and I built a nice toolshed out of lipstick containers. I
don't paint my house anymore; I give it a powder base and then add rouge.
You have a weak spot, too. Advertisers will figure out how to identify your
weak spot and target it. Gullibility will reach heights we never dreamed
possible.

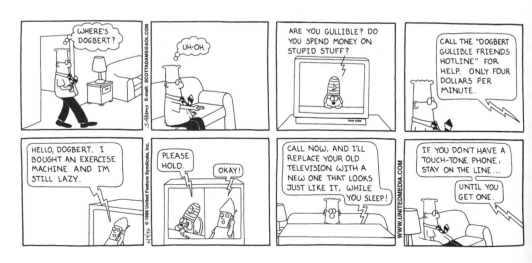

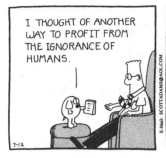

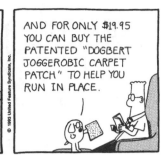

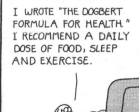

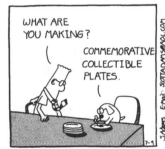

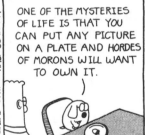

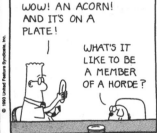

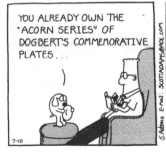

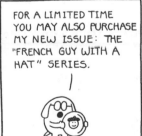

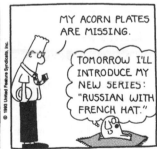

In the future, it will be totally unnecessary to have an actual product in order to sell it. Good advertisements will whip people into a buying frenzy. All you need is a good demo and a complete absence of social conscience.

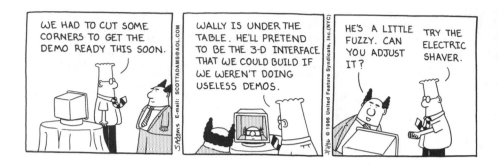

SPIDERWEB MARKETING STRATEGY

When customers find out that a product is terrible they try to avoid paying for it. This can be a real problem for the companies who are trying to sell terrible products. That's why smart companies who provide terrible products have found ways to force you to continue to pay for things you don't want. I call it the "spiderweb marketing strategy." Once they get your credit card number, they have you. The spiderweb technique involves making it so difficult to cancel the product or service that it's easier to just keep it. These are the most effective spiderweb tricks.

How to Prevent Customers from Canceling Your Product or Service

- Have poor phone support so it takes hours to reach a human being who will process the cancellation.

- Print no phone number on your bills or user manual.

- Have penalties for early withdrawal.

- Require the customer to mail the item back before a certain time or else they have to pay for it. (Combine this with the next tip.)

- Make sure the original shipping materials self-destruct when the product is opened. Don't include a mailing address or any other information about how to return the product.

- Underbid the competitors and then, after the customer is committed, say, "Oops, you really need to buy more stuff to make this work. Did I forget to mention that?"

Did you ever wonder why banks have penalties for early withdrawal on some types of accounts? Do you think their computers use more electricity to process certain types of withdrawals? Or maybe there's an obscure banking law that requires banks to screw the consumer a certain number of times per month to remain accredited. Whatever the reason—and I'm sure it's *very* convincing—other industries will jump on that gravy train in the future.

I imagine my dry cleaner telling me why I have to pay a steep penalty if I ever decide to use another dry cleaner. I'll demand an explanation, and he'll say it's a dry-cleaning regulation. He'll exhibit mock frustration with the system and explain how he's just as much a victim as I am. He'll blame the "home office" and politicians in general. All the other dry cleaners will catch wind of this scheme and start doing the same thing. You'll never be able to switch dry cleaners again.

I pay for an online service that I don't use anymore. The charge shows up on my credit card every month. On a per day basis, it's only about thirty cents. I figure it would take about half an hour to find the phone number for customer service, find my account number, work my way through their audiotex menu options, and cancel the service by phone. It's never worth the time. Every day, by putting that task off, I effectively "buy" thirty minutes of time for myself. I will be paying for the online service as long as my time is worth more than a penny a minute. They have me in their spider-web until retirement. By then I will have paid them about $5,000. I'm the perfect customer.

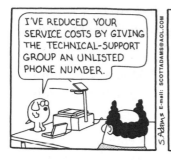

Panel 1: I'VE REDUCED YOUR SERVICE COSTS BY GIVING THE TECHNICAL-SUPPORT GROUP AN UNLISTED PHONE NUMBER.

Panel 2: AND A FLAW IN YOUR PRODUCT DISABLES THE CUSTOMER'S E-MAIL; THEY CAN'T EVEN WRITE TO YOU FOR HELP!

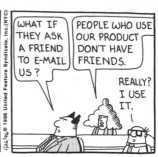

Panel 3: WHAT IF THEY ASK A FRIEND TO E-MAIL US? / PEOPLE WHO USE OUR PRODUCT DON'T HAVE FRIENDS. / REALLY? I USE IT.

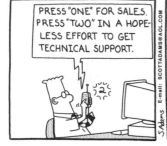

Panel 4: PRESS "ONE" FOR SALES. PRESS "TWO" IN A HOPELESS EFFORT TO GET TECHNICAL SUPPORT.

Panel 5: PRESS "ONE" FOR ANSWERS TO QUESTIONS YOU DON'T HAVE. PRESS "TWO" IF YOU'RE GULLIBLE AND OPTIMISTIC.

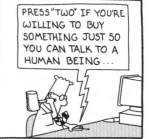

Panel 6: PRESS "TWO" IF YOU'RE WILLING TO BUY SOMETHING JUST SO YOU CAN TALK TO A HUMAN BEING...

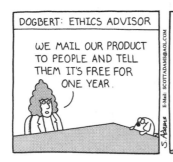

Panel 7: DOGBERT: ETHICS ADVISOR / WE MAIL OUR PRODUCT TO PEOPLE AND TELL THEM IT'S FREE FOR ONE YEAR.

Panel 8: THEN WE START NAILING THEM WITH HIGH FEES BECAUSE THEY'LL FORGET THE PROCEDURE FOR RETURNING THE PRODUCT. THEY'RE TRAPPED.

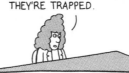

Panel 9: SO, DID YOU HAVE SOME ETHICS ADVICE? / NO. I ASKED YOU HERE SO I CAN RETURN YOUR STUPID PRODUCT.

My favorite spiderweb marketing trick involves selling a complicated and expensive system and then later telling the customer he needs to buy more stuff to make it work. The poor Induhvidual has no choice, because the alternative is to admit defeat and start over with another vendor who will probably pull the same trick. This technique works especially well when combined with a lease contract, because the lease adds its own penalties for changes. The typical lease contract is so complicated it creates spontaneous brain tumors if you read it carefully, so it's fairly foolproof.

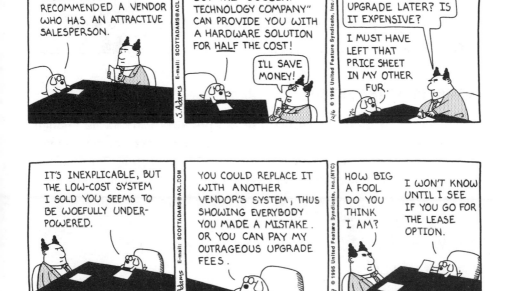

The spiderweb marketing we've seen so far is somewhat passive. The customer has to blunder into the service and get stuck before it can work. I expect things to get worse for the consumer.

PREDICTION 44

In the future, companies will make aggressive products that resist any attempts at refunds or cancellation while actively trying to take more of your money.

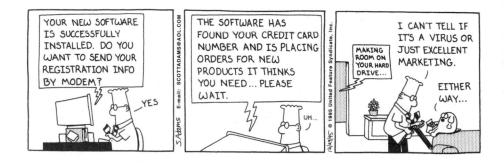

MARKETS OF THE FUTURE

Today most new products fail because the producer can't locate enough customers. Sometimes that's because the product is a piece of crap; sometimes it's because the company isn't successful at marketing. Those problems will go away in the future, due to the following important trends:

1. More Induhviduals are born every day.

2. We're getting better at identifying them.

3. Induhviduals have money, temporarily.

To illustrate my point, let's say you develop a ridiculous product that no intelligent person would want or need. For example, let's say the product is a "house sweater"—literally, a big, wool, knitted sweater that fits over your entire house with the chimney sticking through the neck opening.

If you tried to sell this product today, you'd sell maybe three of them: One to an eccentric person who thought it would be different, one to a person who is simply stupid, and a third to someone who ordered it accidentally and was embarrassed to return it. That would be your entire sales of the house sweater before you ran out of money and closed the company.

There are many more potential buyers out there—people just like the three who bought it—but there's no economical way to reach them. Television advertising is too expensive, because advertising rates are based on the number of people watching regardless of how many of them would ever want a house sweater. And there's no specialty magazine to advertise in—no *House Sweater Quarterly*. There are no house sweater interest groups meeting weekly. It seems hopeless from a marketing standpoint— at least today.

In the future, these problems will be solved. Computer and Internet technology will be able to track everyone's bizarre interests and mental defects. Our house sweater company will be able to buy a customer list of all the eccentric, stupid, and timid people who own houses and have extra cash. They'll be able to market directly to the people who are most likely to buy the product, and that can be very cost-effective.

PREDICTION 45

In the future, it will be easy to find customers who are gullible enough to buy any product, no matter how worthless and stupid it is.

Computers on the Internet will cleverly monitor the transactions of every human on Earth and combine this data with information from credit card companies, stores, and other public records until there is a complete profile of just how gullible you are and in what ways you are most easily duped. We're all gullible about something or other. Currently, we can conceal our gullibilities most of the time. In the future, we won't be able to keep it a secret. That information will be available to anyone who wants it.

There won't be any customer list of people who want house sweaters, of course, since the product didn't exist before, but you can draw inferences from the other behaviors of consumers. For example, the people who buy abdominal exercise machines to lose weight are potential customers for the house sweater, but those names are going to cost you more, since everyone will want a shot at that group.

And more good news for House Sweater, Inc.: The sheer size of the world population guarantees a virtually endless supply of new eccentric, stupid, and timid customer prospects. In fact, there will be so many new prospects that the company will never be burdened with the need to satisfy current customers. It will be cheaper to find new customers and leave them unsatisfied, too. And if you combine this with the spiderweb marketing technique, you can get people to not only keep their house sweaters, but to sign up to receive a ball of yarn every month too for an additional $29.95 apiece.

Once you've bought your list of eccentric, stupid, timid people (let's call them the EST market segment), you can begin to craft your marketing plan.

With this sort of product, you might want to convince people to buy it before telling them what it is. It sounds hard, but insurance companies do this all the time. If you've ever purchased insurance, you know that you can't get an insurance company to tell you what your policy covers until *after* you buy the insurance. Later, after your check clears (because they can't trust you), the insurance company will send you an incomprehensible document. The document will describe what you just bought in a way that is calculated to make you feel stupid and powerless. Eventually, you realize that your best strategy is to mail the insurance company whatever money they ask for and hope for the best.

You can also use this strategy for the house sweater.

TEN

GOOD AND BAD JOBS OF THE FUTURE

Young people often ask me how they should prepare for the job markets of the future. Obviously, they're trying to steal all of my career secrets so they can take my job and leave me homeless and broke. I generally try to steer young people toward a life of crime in the inner cities, because I never go to the inner cities and I figure that's as good a place as any for crime.

If a young person is hesitant to take my advice, I can usually make my case by pointing out the many disadvantages of the alternatives. I'll do that in this chapter, thereby reducing the need for me to speak directly with young people who are future criminals.

The first thing that young people need to realize is that the concepts of "career" and "job security" are a bit dated.

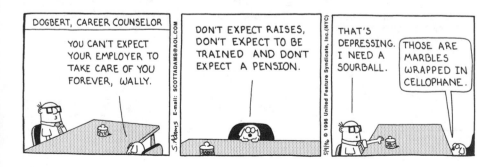

In the future, most people's jobs will involve scrambling around like frightened chipmunks trying to find the next paycheck in an endless string of unrelated short-term jobs. But since "Frightened Chipmunk" doesn't look very impressive on a business card, people will call themselves entrepreneurs, consultants, and independent contractors.

It will get harder and harder to generate good small talk at parties. Someone will ask you what you do for a living, and you'll have to give a vague answer like, "I work in Cleveland," and hope the interrogation ends. As a rule, if it takes more than two words to describe what you do for a living, it's not a "career" in the classic sense of the word. Doctor is a career. Lawyer is a career. You do not have a career if you describe it as, "I'm working on a meeting to see someone about a project that involves a potential consulting assignment."

If you were foolish enough go to college and major in one of the soft arts, such as journalism, English literature or music, you might have a bit of a shock coming. At best, those majors are excellent preparation for jobs that involve removing wine corks and condoms from the swimming pools of people who studied computer science. And even that is seasonal work.

I'm probably overgeneralizing. There are plenty of other jobs you can get if you have a degree in the squishy subjects, as long as you're not burdened by a lot of excess human dignity.

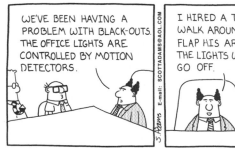 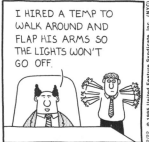 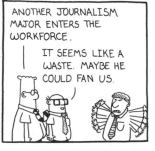

If you are one of the few lucky people who attended a big-name school, things will be completely different. You'll be highly recruited by large companies and put on the fast track, unless of course you're ugly. The attractive graduates of big-name schools earn obscene salaries, buy expensive stuff, and die in freak accidents. The ugly ones enter academia. Either way it's tragic.

Another career trap you want to avoid is becoming an "exempt" employee, sometimes also referred to as "salaried" or, more colloquially, "gullible."

Exempt employees are paid the same no matter how many hours they work. Companies can increase their earnings by making employees work additional hours for free under the threat of downsizing. This is what we call a bad situation for employees. Ideally, you want the kind of job where your employer has very little temptation to work you until every last bit of life has been drained out of your flabby, decaying body.

Some clever employers will try to disguise their no-overtime-pay scam by dressing it up as something glamorous. When I was hired at Pacific Bell in 1986, they told me I was a "manager." It even said so on my business card. I kept thinking that the people who reported to me must be hiding, because I never met any of them. The trick, as I later learned, is that managers weren't eligible for overtime pay. Eventually, the only thing I managed was—and this took some effort—to resist strangling the Induhviduals who came up with this plan.

I complained bitterly about this situation until my boss agreed to change my title from "manager" to "supreme commander of cubicle 4S700R." I still didn't get paid for overtime, but at least I had the respect of my peers. Well, I would have had their respect, if not for the quality of my work and my insistence that they salute.

There was a time, long ago, when you could park your lazy butt in a large benevolent company and reasonably expect to retire from it in thirty years as a bitter, broken shell of your former self, living out your miserable life on a subsistence retirement income. But things won't be so easy in the future. Now every employee can expect to change jobs up to 7,000 times (I'm guessing on the actual figure). In such an environment, it's a good idea to have a well-planned educational foundation. In particular, I recommend avoiding any ethics classes.

PREDICTION 46

In the future, the most important career skill will be a lack of ethics.

If you acquire too many ethics in college, it will be a severe drain on your earnings potential. The most important corporate skill in the future will be the ability to make sure your co-workers get downsized before you do. Some people might try to optimize their chances of surviving a downsizing by working hard, but as the name implies, that would be both "hard" and "work."

You can predict an impending wave of downsizing by looking for signals in the environment. Those signals might include a company merger, a bad earnings report, a new CEO nicknamed "chainsaw," or really just about any old thing. It doesn't take much to trigger a wave of downsizing these days—a paper jam in the photocopier or somebody forgets to bring donuts and poof, there goes another thousand co-workers.

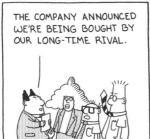
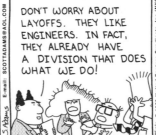
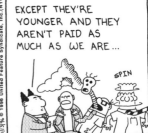

If you notice any of the signals of downsizing, that is when all of the teamwork of the past pays off. When you're a team, you work closely with one another. And when you work closely with other people, you learn all of their heinous faults. This would be a good time to let everyone else know about them.

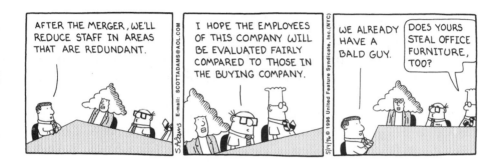

Another good skill to pick up in college is mime. If you join a big company, you'll spend a surprising number of hours totally motionless, and you might as well turn it into something artistic. Try pretending your cubicle has an invisible door or ceiling and you're a powerless employee trapped inside. It's a stretch, but you can do it. You can entertain yourself for hours this way. But make sure you don't try to entertain other people, because I've noticed a real stigma against cubicle mimes.

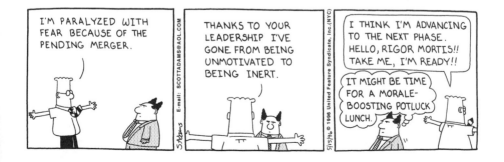

Now that I've thoroughly explored the educational needs of the future, let me turn my attention to some specific jobs you will want to either carefully consider or avoid in the future.

MOTHERS, DON'T LET YOUR CHILDREN GROW UP TO BE VENDORS

The typical employee of the typical company is a bitter and powerless person who longs for any opportunity to spread the pain. There are few opportunities to do that at the bottom of the corporate hierarchy, so employees naturally look to the one class of people who are paid to take their abuse: vendors.

Vendors are people who make a living by enduring an endless barrage of rude and degrading treatment at the hands of their customers. The vendor who endures the most abuse is considered "flexible" and gets the sale. It's that simple.

Some vendors will go out of their way to invent their own abuse in order to win the abuse contest. They'll offer to loan you products they know you'll lose or ignore. They'll send you endless copies of product information no matter how many times you lose it. They'll offer to drive across town to answer a question that could be answered on the phone. If they're motivated enough, you can sometimes get them to poke themselves with sharp pencils just for fun.

Vendors try to be "part of the team," and they are usually the best teammates you could possibly have, because you can abuse them and they won't screw you during the next downsizing. You can cancel meetings with them, insult their products, accuse them of lying, and generally treat them like the stuff that's hard to get out of the cracks in your sneakers.

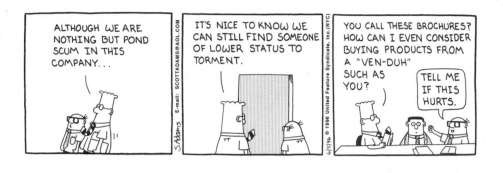

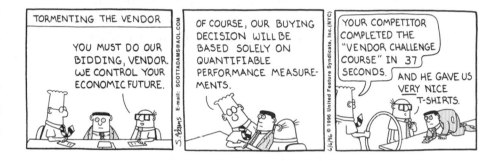

Although the job conditions are dismal, vendors can make a lot of
money. If they are clever enough to cultivate relationships with (i.e., bribe)
senior management, they will be in a position to exact revenge on the
lower-level employees who tormented them. If you think you have the
type of personality to be a successful vendor, you might want to explore
career options in related fields first:

Related Occupations

- Hit man.

- Prostitute.

- Sadomasochist.

- Movie producer.

PROCUREMENT

The job of procurement isn't as sexy as it sounds. It mostly involves pre-venting people from getting stuff they need to do their jobs. The primary qualifications for a career in procurement include this sort of thing:

- Long hairy arms.

- Low forehead.

- Inability to grasp the big picture.

Most dinosaurs worked in procurement before they went into hiding. Many of them starved to death while waiting for a purchase order for edible vegetation. Others evolved into birds, primarily in the penguin family. Those who survived have carried on the tradition.

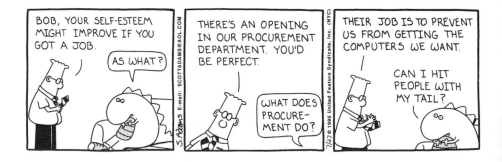

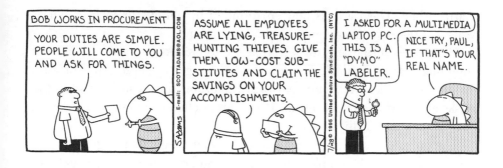

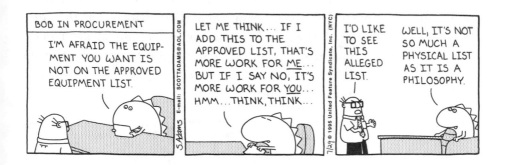

TEMP

For the young people who are preparing for their futures by watching television, there is an exciting field you should consider. It's called being a "temp," which is short for "I'm *temp*ted to have a real job, but not enthusiastic about the concept."

Companies hire temp workers for much the same reasons that NASA used chimps in its early rocket testing. It's a little known fact, but the people at NASA hate chimps. The whole "race to the moon" thing was just an excuse to get rid of chimps by sending them into space attached to huge, combustible devices. The media covered the first few chimp flights, but then turned their attention to the flights piloted by the humans that NASA hated. (The term "astronaut" is Latin for "let's send this Induhvidual into space.") Meanwhile, NASA quietly launched millions of chimps into low

Earth orbits. The Earth is now surrounded by chimps in rockets. That's why your television sometimes has bad reception.

Companies hire temps for jobs that are too hideous to give to someone they might grow fond of. There are no shortages of these types of jobs. Every day, millions of temps perform important duties such as sitting at desks and staring straight ahead. If you are a child of television, as I was, you are already qualified for this job.

The only downside as far as I can tell is that temps do not get as much respect as the regular employees. And the regular employees don't get any. As a temp, nobody will ask your name or offer to introduce you to the rest of the office. People will walk up to you and abruptly bark orders that are full of arcane acronyms. You will have no idea what they are talking about, but that's okay. No matter what you do, it won't affect your career as a temp. In fact, if you do something that causes a gigantic explosion or mass hysteria, at least it breaks up your day.

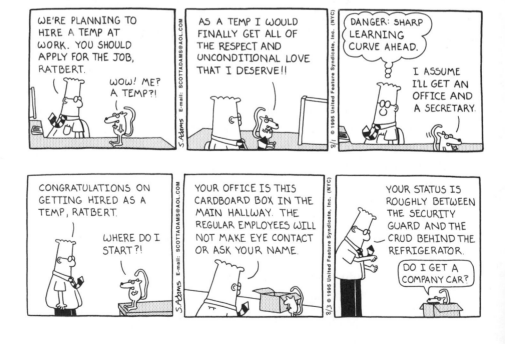

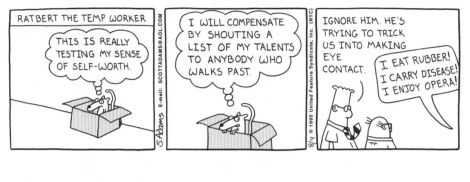

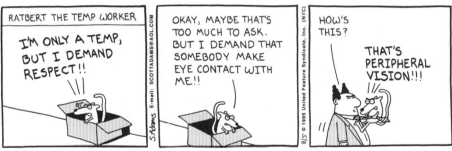

ACCOUNTING, AUDITING, AND DENTISTRY

Accounting, auditing, and dentistry are all excellent career choices for people who don't like other people but aren't coordinated enough to beat those other people up.

If you can't decide which of the three choices is best for you, use this handy test: Ask yourself whether you prefer to hear people scream in pain (choose dentistry), scream in frustration (choose accounting), or scream in a prison shower (choose auditing).

The accounting profession is an excellent way to get a lot of time by yourself. At a party, try saying, "I'm an accountant. Today was an interesting day." Notice how quickly you're standing alone.

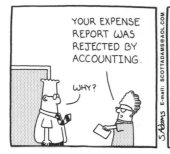

YOUR EXPENSE REPORT WAS REJECTED BY ACCOUNTING.

WHY?

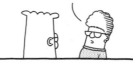

BECAUSE THE EMPTINESS OF THEIR SHALLOW LIVES MAKES THEM WANT TO HURT OTHERS IN ORDER TO VALIDATE THEIR PATHETIC EXISTENCE.

CAN YOU HELP ME CLEAR THIS UP?

TO BE HONEST, I'M KINDA BUYING IN TO THEIR PHILOSOPHY.

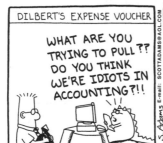

IF IT'S OKAY, I'LL HOLD ONTO MY SOUL WHILE I VISIT THE ACCOUNTING DEPARTMENT.

SOUL CHECK

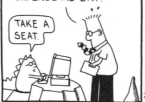

I CAME TO ANSWER YOUR QUESTIONS ABOUT MY EXPENSE REPORT.

TAKE A SEAT.

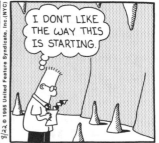

I DON'T LIKE THE WAY THIS IS STARTING.

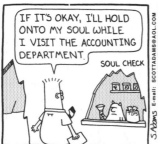

DILBERT'S EXPENSE VOUCHER

WHAT ARE YOU TRYING TO PULL?? DO YOU THINK WE'RE IDIOTS IN ACCOUNTING?!!

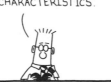

NO, I SWEAR, I THINK YOU'RE SMART BUT SADISTIC TROLLS WITH MANY HUMANOID CHARACTERISTICS.

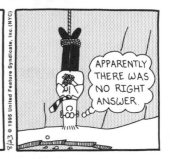

APPARENTLY THERE WAS NO RIGHT ANSWER.

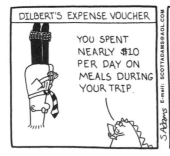

DILBERT'S EXPENSE VOUCHER

YOU SPENT NEARLY $10 PER DAY ON MEALS DURING YOUR TRIP.

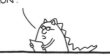

THE TRAVEL GUIDELINES REQUIRE YOU TO STUN A PIGEON WITH YOUR BRIEFCASE ON THE WAY TO THE HOTEL THEN FRY IT UP ON YOUR TRAVEL IRON.

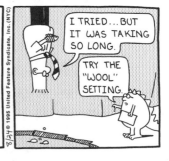

I TRIED... BUT IT WAS TAKING SO LONG.

TRY THE "WOOL" SETTING.

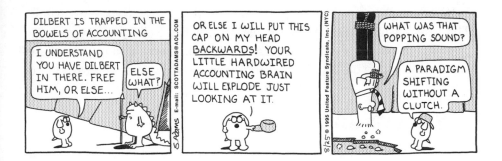

Sometimes accountants can get more respect by saying they work in the finance department. Finance is a sexier word than accounting, but the work tends to be similar, as in this example:

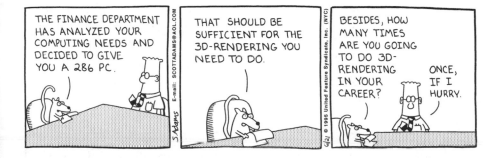

Auditors get more respect and more bribes than accountants. That's because auditors are relatively more dangerous. Auditors are generally plucked from the ranks of accountants who had very bad childhood experiences. Those accountants who don't go on to become serial killers have a good chance of becoming successful auditors.

Dentists are the people who filled out their career aptitude tests in high school and checked the box that says, "Would you enjoy reaching into helpless people's mouths with power tools and causing excruciating pain?" The people who said yes to that question either become prison interrogators in Third World countries or dentists. I recommend either one of those careers, because you always have someone else to take your frustrations out on.

VENTURE CAPITALIST

The very best job I can think of is venture capitalist. Not only does it sound great at parties, but you're expected to fail 90 percent of the time. I mean no disrespect to venture capitalists when I say this, but a hamster with Alzheimer's could make those kinds of numbers. It's good work if you can get it.

For those of you who are unfamiliar with the venture capital occupation, it mostly involves taking rich people's money and giving it to small businesses that soon become bankrupt. Once in a while, one of those small companies becomes huge, and the venture capitalists get rich and buy four-wheel-drive vehicles for no particular reason. I'm leaving out some details that involve eating, drinking, and laughing at morons behind their backs, but I think you get the gist of it.

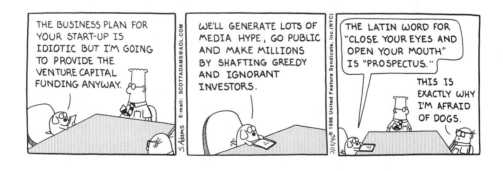

DOGBERT, VENTURE CAPITALIST
YOU'LL USE YOUR TECHNICAL EXPERTISE AND I'LL DO THE BUSINESS STUFF. SIGN HERE.
E-Mail: SCOTTADAMS@AOL.COM
S. Adams
SINCE YOU'RE THE INVENTOR OF THE TECHNOLOGY, YOU'LL GET 100% OF THE SPECIAL DECORATIVE NON-EQUITY STOCK. I'LL SETTLE FOR ALL THE COMMON STOCK.
© 1995 United Feature Syndicate, Inc.
1-12
I HOPE WE CAN AVOID THE TENSION THAT SOME PARTNERS EXPERIENCE.
GIVE ME MY PEN, YOU MISCREANT.

DOGBERT, VENTURE CAPITALIST
MY IDEA IS TO DEVELOP A WORD PROCESSING PROGRAM FOR WINDOWS.
E-Mail: SCOTTADAMS@AOL.COM
S. Adams
THAT'S AN INTERESTING CONCEPT. I WONDER IF TWENTY DOLLARS WOULD BE ENOUGH.
© 1995 United Feature Syndicate, Inc.
1-13
TO START A SOFTWARE COMPANY?
NO, TO PAY OUR WAITRESS TO BEAT YOU WITH A LOAF OF FRENCH BREAD.

DOGBERT, VENTURE CAPITALIST
I'LL INVEST UP TO FIVE MILLION DOLLARS IF YOU'LL AGREE TO SOME STANDARD CONDITIONS.
E-Mail: SCOTTADAMS@AOL.COM
S. Adams
I WILL BE CHAIRMAN OF THE BOARD AND OWN 99% OF THE COMPANY. YOU WILL WORK FOR FREE AND WASH MY CAR TWICE A WEEK.
© 1995 United Feature Syndicate, Inc.
1-14
CAN I MOW YOUR LAWN INSTEAD OF WASHING YOUR CAR?
YOU'RE A TOUGH BARGAINER, BUT I PREFER MULTIMEDIA DEVELOPERS FOR MY GARDENING NEEDS.

RECORDS RETENTION

The corporate world is full of jobs that you will never hear about except by reading informative books like this one. Some of these jobs are as close to Nirvana as work can be. My favorite nearly-heaven job is something called records retention.

Most companies generate tons of documents that nobody needs to read yet seem too important to throw away. Employees don't have room to keep all the documents at their desks. The solution is something called records retention. In theory, employees send documents to a person who stores those documents in a huge warehouse, available for retrieval when necessary.

It's possible that this sometimes happens exactly as planned, but I know that if I had that job, I would move a Dumpster into the office with a sign that said, PLACE DOCUMENTS FOR STORAGE INSIDE. Then I'd never go to work again. The ugly truth is that almost nobody goes looking for a document that has been sent to the warehouse. If someone does, you can say it was lost or blame it on the temp whose name you can't remember. Most jobs in corporate life have no value to the economy, but there are scant few that so aggressively ignore any attempt at even appearing useful.

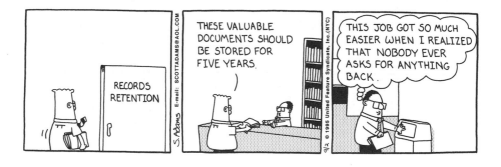

GET PAID TO CRITICIZE OTHERS

If there is one thing you should always seek in a job, it's the opportunity to criticize people who are more skilled than you are. This kind of work is both satisfying and easy.

Good jobs in this vein include newspaper and magazine columnist. If you're a young person who is accustomed to being selected last for teams, these are excellent jobs for you.

As you read this sentence, somewhere there is a columnist writing an article about how much this book sucks. As I type this sentence using the dominant word processing software on the planet Earth, a technology columnist is giving a speech about how bad it is. As the secretary of defense is poring through top-secret intelligence reports to figure out how to keep the planet safe, a writer is researching an important story about how the secretary pays his maid.

I think you can see who has the easier job in these examples.

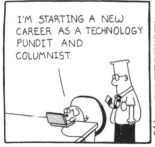
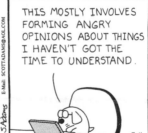
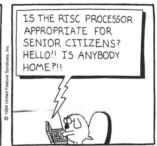
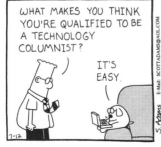
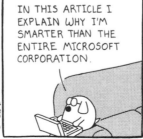
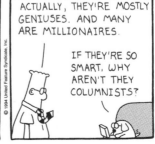

If you want to be at the top of the criticism food chain, become a publisher or an editor. In those jobs, you will be in a position to criticize not only the people who do real work, but also the people who criticize those people. It simply doesn't get any better than that.

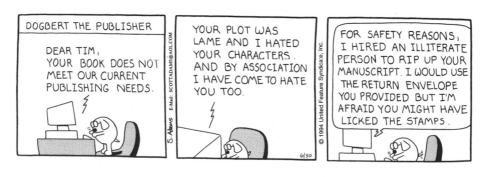

ELEVEN

SOCIAL STUFF

POVERTY

I don't know why everyone says poverty can't be eliminated. The solution is obvious to me. All it takes is what the bankers call the "miracle of compound interest."

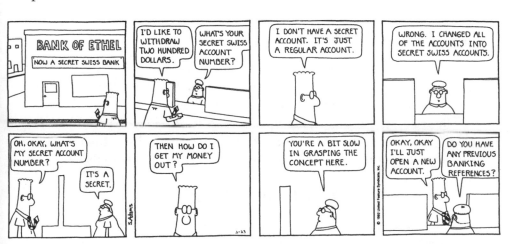

This requires a long-term approach to the problem, but it's fairly foolproof if you're patient. All you do is give each poor person one dollar. There are only about 5 billion poor people, so this is quite affordable as a percentage of the worldwide GNP. That dollar is deposited in a special bank account for each of the poor people with the idea that it stays there for generations collecting interest. The number of poor people doubles every twenty years, but the value of money doubles every ten years, assuming it is well invested, so the gap will close.

In 4,000 years, the descendants of the poor people will be allowed to go to the bank and ask for their money. The bank will inform them that the dollar was taken in fees 4,000 years ago, and the balance of all their accounts is zero. At this point, the poor people will kill the bankers and steal all the money in the banks, thus ending poverty completely.

I'm surprised nobody has suggested it before.

PREDICTION 47

In the future, poverty will be eliminated, along with the people who are hoarding all the money.

THE AGE OF CONSENT

A hundred years ago, the legal age of consent for a woman was ten years old. Now it's eighteen. When I was a teenager in New York State, the legal age for drinking was eighteen. Now it's twenty-one.

The legal ages are creeping up, because it's obvious that the people below those ages are complete morons and can't handle sex and liquor. But what about the people over the legal ages? How bright are they?

True Story (Really. I was there.)

A secretary for a large bank was engaged to be married. She was nineteen and completely uninformed about the various methods of birth control. Her co-workers sat her down and explained the rhythm method, because that was the only method allowed by her religion. They described how she should count the days from her last period to determine when she was most likely to be fertile.

She listened intently and asked only one question, "Do you only count business days?"

Every time the legal age of something gets moved higher, we discover that the people just above the legal age are no smarter than the people just below it. The obvious solution is to keep increasing the age limits until we find the age where people become smart and responsible.

PREDICTION 48

In the future, the age of consent for sex and liquor
will be raised to 120.

This will not have any impact on the amount of actual sex and drinking in the world, but at least we'll know our lawmakers weren't sitting idly by while the world went to hell.

CRIME

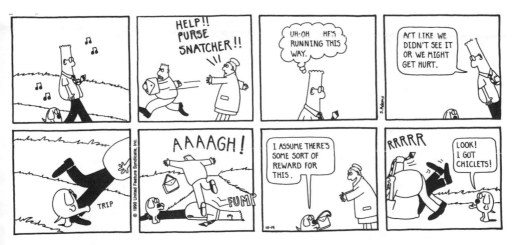

PREDICTION 49

In the future, new technology will allow police to solve 100 percent
of all crimes. The bad news is that we'll realize 100 percent of the
population are criminals, including the police.

You might be an undetected criminal already. Review this list to determine whether you're getting away with something:

Have You Committed Any of These Crimes?

- Speeding in your car?

- Using office supplies for personal business?

- Making personal phone calls from the phone at work?

- Violating copyright law?

- "Borrowing" a *Dilbert* book from a dim-witted co-worker?

- Cheating on your taxes?

- Taking drugs?

- Operating a motor vehicle while legally drunk?

- Drinking liquor as a minor?

- Having sex with a seventeen-year-old?

- Threatening to "kill someone"?

- Slapping someone?

- Using a scanner to overhear your neighbor's phone conversations?

- Recording a conversation without someone's permission?

- Sending personal e-mail messages from work?

- Exaggerating expenses on an expense report?

- Lying to a highway patrolman?

- Littering?

- Making lewd comments at work?

- Fishing without a license?

You might argue that, although you have done some of those things in the past, you aren't doing any of them now. I'm sure that's true, unless you stole this book and you're running from the police while you read it. But most convicted criminals aren't committing crimes AT THIS VERY MOMENT either. There are two big differences between the average criminal and you:

1. The average criminal got caught.

2. The average criminal's crimes are "bigger."

In the future, the crimes you commit won't seem "little," because you'll get caught every single time. You'll get a ticket EVERY TIME you exceed the speed limit. The fines will exceed your income, and you'll become a scofflaw. There will be a warrant for your arrest. You'll lose your license and your car insurance, but you'll drive anyway. Then you'll get caught driving without a license or insurance. Eventually, you'll be sent to prison for life or possibly executed. (The courts are getting tougher on repeat offenders.)

If you don't believe everyone is breaking the law, look at your politicians. Virtually all major politicians seem to get caught doing something illegal. There are four explanations for this observation:

Possible Reasons Why All Politicians Seem to Be Crooks

1. Crooks are the only ones who run for office.

2. Politics turns people into criminals.

3. All politicians are being framed.

4. Every person on Earth is a crook, but the only people we check out carefully are politicians.

There's no reason to believe that crooks are the only people who run for office. And I can't believe public service turns honest people into criminals. And I can't believe that all honest politicians can be framed so easily without the people who do the framing ever getting caught themselves. The most logical explanation for the politician/crook phenomenon is that all people are criminals and only the politicians are watched closely enough to get caught.

We like to think the world is composed of honest people on one side and crooks on the other, but all the evidence points to the theory that everyone is a crook. Some people are dumb enough to get caught and some aren't. Consider this true story:

True Story

A co-worker once told me he had a theory about why there were shortages of water in some parts of the world. His theory was that people are drinking it all.

I'll bet he's in jail now. He obviously isn't bright enough to avoid detection for whatever crimes he committed. I have to assume he's sitting in a cell somewhere guzzling water out of the prison sink and yelling, "THEY'LL PAY! THEY'LL ALL PAY!"

Eventually, everyone will be in jail except Marilyn vos Savant, the world's smartest human. She's the only person on Earth who will be smart enough to get away with everything. She'll complain constantly about the taxes she pays to keep the whole planet incarcerated, but on some level she will realize it's her own responsibility, because she's in charge of the planet.

The incarceration of the entire planet will come about due to a chain of events beginning with an increase in terrorism. Here's how it will play out.

At the moment, you still need to be a fairly well-informed terrorist in order to do any serious damage. But what happens when any disgruntled Induhvidual can build a weapon of mass destruction by ordering the parts through magazines? When we reach that point—and you know we will—anyone in a bad mood will be a threat to world security.

In the future, after a few cities are annihilated by miffed figure skaters who think the judges were biased, there will be a spirited debate about whether people should give up their privacy in return for greater security. Both sides will make excellent arguments, but no one will be persuaded.

After a few more metropolitan areas are obliterated, the argument will eventually be won by the people who favor safety over privacy. By that time, our technology will have reached a point where all crimes can be solved as long as we're willing to give up privacy.

There are several evolving technologies that will make it possible to detect nearly 100 percent of all crimes. I'll describe a few. These predictions are based on technology that already exists at some stage of development.

Artificial Noses

There's already a technology that can detect almost anything with an odor and match it against a known smell. Initially, it will be used to sniff for bombs at airports.

A bloodhound can detect a person's scent and follow it hours after the crime, distinguishing it from all other scents. The artificial nose machines could someday be that accurate and portable. Police could grab an air sample from the crime scene and use it to track suspects hours after the crime. Or they could use the technology to "sniff" suspects out of a lineup.

Repeat offenders would have their scents on file—like fingerprints—so computers could find an instant match to the scent at the crime scene. Courts would eventually accept "sniff evidence" like they accept fingerprints and DNA evidence.

DNA Matches

It's almost impossible to enter a room and commit a crime without leaving microscopic pieces of your hair, skin, blood, or saliva. Under our current system, this only helps police after they have a suspect to test. But in the future, if people give up personal privacy for better protection, every citizen will have their DNA pattern, scent, and fingerprints on file with the police.

Investigators will be able to vacuum a crime scene, run it through the DNA analyzer, and get the name and address of every person who has been there lately.

Ubiquitous Video

Many crimes are already being captured on surveillance videos and personal video cameras. There are only two reasons we don't put cameras everywhere: cost and privacy.

Both of those obstacles will go away. The cost of cameras is dropping every day, and our willingness to pay for crime prevention is increasing. Cost will not be an issue.

People will be willing to give up some privacy for increased security. One town in California already has video cameras at virtually all public locations. People got used to it.

I predict we'll have cameras at all *private* locations as well, including your car and all rooms of your house. The cameras will run all the time and record the images in an encrypted form that only law enforcement officers can decipher—but only with a court order. That's similar to the way law enforcement now gains access to any of your personal records or phone conversations (except for the encryption part). You won't like it, but you'll get used to it.

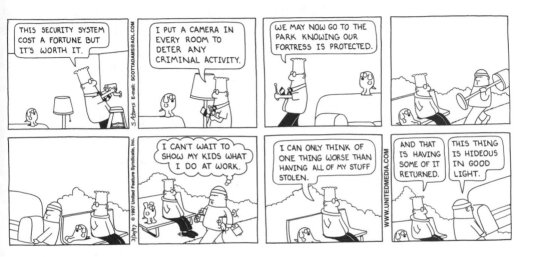

When all criminals get caught, jail overcrowding will become the big issue. But that's Marilyn vos Savant's problem, not ours. We'll be in jail. I just hope she doesn't favor the death penalty, because that will be the most cost-effective solution and I know she can do the math.

NEWS IN THE FUTURE

When the Unabomber was captured, I mentioned something about it to a friend. She stared blankly at me. It was the biggest news of the year, and she had never heard of the Unabomber. Wilting under my barrage of intense questioning, she confessed that a few years ago she decided to make a conscious effort to avoid all news sources. She believes the news is depressing and has no bearing on her life. I was shocked and dismayed, especially when I realized she's right. I've noticed several other friends who are also pursuing an aggressive strategy of ignoring all news. When I say aggressive, I mean they make a conscious effort to avoid even *accidental* exposure to news.

What caused this trend?

Somehow, without anybody really noticing, the news changed from events that affect us—such as major wars and stock market crashes—to stuff that doesn't affect most of us at all, like athletes slaying their wives.

Governments have figured out how to control the big bone-headed catastrophes that made news in the past. These days, you never hear about a cow kicking over a lantern causing a major metropolitan area to be engulfed in flames. Now, thanks to government regulations, all the cows use flashlights and nobody gets hurt.

Rich guys used to be able to manipulate the stock market and make huge profits at the expense of smaller investors. It was big news when the small investors discovered they'd been screwed. Now there are many safeguards against the small investor ever finding out how much he's getting screwed. That means the financial news is limited to interviews with bald guys who try to guess why the market moved ten points today. It's not really "news" in the sense that it has any relevance.

War isn't as newsworthy as it used to be either. All the big countries with impressive weapons can't figure out a good reason to point them at each other. This makes it very difficult for the generals to design realistic war games:

War Games Planning

General: Let's assume that Holland attacks NATO . . .

Captain: I think Holland is part of NATO.

General: It is? Damn. Who's *not* on our side yet?

Captain: Umm . . . Switzerland?

General: Great. We'll kick their little lederhosen butts!

Social problems are reported as statistics that rise and fall for no apparent reason. The only fun part is watching politicians trying to distribute blame without accidentally using the phrase, "I sure hope you voters *are* as dumb as you look!"

Economic news is too abstract for the average viewer. It's hard to be excited about news when you can't even tell if it's good news or bad news. The value of the yen is up? Uh-oh, now what do I do?

The occasional serial killer story is interesting, but the likelihood of the serial killer snuffing me personally is so small that that it's hard to get excited about it. Serial killing is a very bad thing, but logically, nine people killed by a serial killer isn't as bad as ten people who are each killed by a separate killer. Serial-killer stories are the most impressive news we have, and they only sound relevant when they're taken out of context. That's the best evidence that news isn't important anymore.

The other clue that all the important stories are gone is the number of news reports about other news reports. This morning I saw a news story about how a tabloid obtained photos of a crime scene. News about the news gatherers is more interesting than whatever they're gathering news about. Could anything be *less* relevant than news about how someone gathered the news about a story that wasn't relevant in the first place?

PREDICTION 50

In the future, more people will actively ignore the news
because it is irrelevant.

I predict that news outlets will try to compensate for the loss of relevant news by focusing on stories that are more shocking and depressing than ever. At least that way they'll get your attention and sell advertising even if the stories aren't "news" in the traditional sense.

This will limit the reporting to a few stories per year about famous people who are killing other famous people. And if there are not enough of those stories to sell advertising slots, the media will do the only responsible thing—they will start to kill famous people themselves. Eventually, the news people will get caught and go to jail, and that will be the end of traditional news outlets.

PREDICTION 51

In the future, the media will kill famous people to generate news that people will care about.

The end of traditional news outlets will not limit people's access to information. Thanks to the ubiquity of video cameras and the Internet, every citizen will be a reporter. If something happens in your neighborhood, you'll tape it, stick it on the Internet with your own commentary, and make it available to the world. Sports commentary and statistics will be generated by fans who enjoy doing it for free. The weather reports will be computer-generated and constantly available by computer, pager, voice mail, and dozens of other sources. All news gathering will be disaggregated.

PREDICTION 52

In the future, everyone will be a news reporter.

People will have access to software that constantly combs the Internet for "small" news that is relevant to them. The software will learn to filter out reports from Induhviduals who constantly post incorrect information. You will still get misleading reports quite often, but that's no different from today.

Some new safeguards will emerge to check the credibility of Induhviduals who post news to the Net. For example, your software will be able to do a sort of "credibility credit check" on any person who posts information to the Internet. It will compare this information to other reports on the same event and automatically highlight any discrepancies. This won't be foolproof, but nothing is.

This new model depends on people being willing to take the time to put information on the Net without the benefit of payment. Why will people do that? They will do it because that's our most basic human nature:

> People like to talk more than they like to listen.

That's why our mouths are much bigger than the combined sizes of our ear holes. (I realize that statement makes no sense, yet it's strangely compelling.)

It is not only unnecessary to pay people to tell you what they know, it's almost impossible to stop them from doing it.

I print my e-mail address in my *Dilbert* comic strip. I get 350 messages a day. Many of them are filled with stories, anecdotes, jokes, reports on *Dilbert* copyright violators, comments, opinions, and a wealth of other useful information. All that the writers ask in return is a reasonable likelihood that I will read the message. (I do my best.)

Look at the explosion of "personal home pages" on the Internet. People spend untold hours populating their personal web pages with information about their hobbies, opinions, favorite music, and loads of other information that nobody asked for.

Bottom line. We are a species that needs no incentive to give away information. The Internet and video technology will make it easy to share what we know with the world. And boy will we share.

PREDICTION 53

In the future, the thing we'll miss most about the traditional "news media" will be the professional reporters asking penetrating questions.

Here are some of the questions I will miss the most.

Penetrating News Media Questions

- "General, can you tell us where you plan the next secret bombing?"
- "Senator, do you really expect to win this election?"
- "Do you think your economic plan will help the country?"
- "Do you feel that you did anything unethical?"
- "Did you really have sex with a penguin?"

PARENT LICENSES

Most Induhviduals end up having children. That's a bit like putting a poodle in the cockpit of the space shuttle and saying, "Let's see what happens."

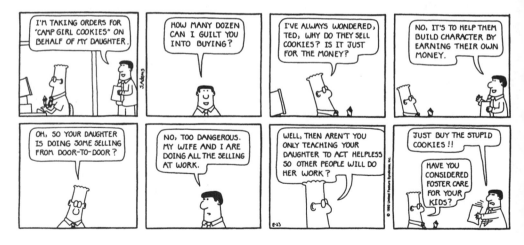

I have to think that raising a human being is one of the most difficult things in the world to do right. But it's one of the few things that people routinely do with no training except for asking the advice of other untrained Induhviduals. This is not a good recipe for success.

You need a license to drive a car. You need a license to catch fish. You need a license to own a dog. But you don't need a license to create a human being. Even children can create other children. There is no minimum-qualification requirement for becoming a parent. If you don't think that's a problem, read this e-mail message I received recently.

Subject: Copy Machine
From: (name withheld)
To: scottadams@aol.com

True Story!
Recently our copier broke down. The repair person came and took the copier apart and was amazed at the extensive paper jam. An Induhvidual walked in and admitted that he had jammed the machine trying to make two-sided copies. The repair person then explained to the Induhvidual very, very slowly that the machine does not have an automatic paper feed; those slits were for ventilation.

It would not surprise me if the paper-jamming Induhvidual went home that night and jammed a pint of baby formula in his baby's ears.

Eventually, we'll figure out that untrained Induhvidual parents are the single biggest cause of all human problems. The government will address it in the usual way.

PREDICTION 54

In the future, parents will have to pass a brief written parent test
in order to get tax credits for dependents.

It won't be a hard test—no more difficult than your driver's test—but I think it will help. Most people know they aren't supposed to pass a school bus if its lights are blinking, but many Induhviduals don't know they can turn their kids into felons, auditors, and rhythmic swimmers just by saying the wrong things. This is a very fixable problem.

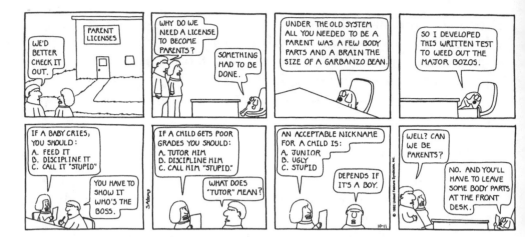

EUTHANASIA

People disagree on the question of whether it should be legal for a person to commit suicide, but people are in favor of getting tough on crime, including more use of the death penalty. Am I the only one who sees an obvious solution here?

Let's make it illegal to threaten yourself and let's make it punishable by death. If you threaten to kill yourself, the state kills you. That way everyone wins.

PREDICTION 55

In the future, it will be illegal to threaten yourself, and
the penalty for doing so will be death.

Then there's the question of whether doctors should be allowed to assist people in dying. It's easy to predict where this debate will go. For doctors, killing people is relatively easy money compared to keeping them alive. Even if the doctor accidentally mixes the wrong combination of lethal drugs and the patient lives, there's always the option of beating the patient with the IV stand—i.e., "alternative medicine."

Doctors have very powerful lobbying groups. The law will change to make assisted suicide legal (for the doctors, not the killee), thus providing an excellent source of income for the medical profession. There will be a spirited ethical debate among doctors, but I think the outcome is predictable.

Doctors already perform many unnecessary surgeries because the money is good. Does anyone really think they wouldn't be willing to kill you if the price was right? The savings in malpractice insurance alone would be worth it, assuming none of the dead people sue for "accidental life."

The market price for assisted suicide is artificially low right now, because Dr. Kevorkian is driving around in an old van doing them for free. As soon as Kevorkian retires, the market will determine a fair price for assisted suicide. Doctors will realize it's easy work compared to appendectomies—and best of all they won't even have to wash their hands first!

PREDICTION 56

In the future, assisted suicide will be a medical specialty practiced by doctors who don't like people.

I think assisted suicide will become a medical specialty. It won't take nearly as much medical training as other specialties. Ten minutes of training should do it.

Patient: My throat is itchy.

Doctor: Hmm, I recommend assisted suicide.

Patient: Suicide?! What if it's just a cold?

Doctor: I wouldn't want to take that chance.

PRIVACY

Last night I was sitting on my couch with a row of pretzels lined up in the crease of my sweatshirt. I carefully selected each pretzel from the lineup based on its aesthetic appeal and salt ratio. I crunched the chosen one slowly and replaced it with another to repeat the search for a best pretzel.

Meanwhile, a national weather report on television was informing me that there were normal temperatures in places I will never visit. At that moment, I realized that I had accidentally discovered a means of keeping my personal life completely private:

I was dangerously boring.

Let's say that someday technology will allow anybody to find out every possible thing about my life. I can compensate by being so uninteresting that nobody could survive the process of snooping on me without lapsing into a coma. Judging from my friends, I don't think I'm the only person who has discovered this sophisticated privacy technique.

PREDICTION 57

In the future, there will be no compelling reason
to invade anyone's privacy.

Celebrities already have total privacy. Everything you read about celebrities is invented by disgruntled nannies and unscrupulous media people. Their true personal lives are a mystery and will stay that way. Personally, I'm grateful that the news about celebrities is fabricated by the media. I don't want to read a story about Barbra Streisand that says she's a very nice person most of the time, but sometimes she gets annoyed when people do bad work. That would describe most of the people I know. I want to hear that Barbra pistol-whipped the pizza delivery boy because he forgot "extra garlic." Now THAT'S entertainment.

Noncelebrities will also have total privacy in the future. The technology for invading your privacy will improve, but the reasons to do so will completely go away. There are three main reasons that people violate your privacy now:

Reasons for Invading Your Privacy

1. To gather marketing data.

2. To commit crimes against you.

3. To get cheap thrills.

Marketing and advertising techniques get better every year. Eventually, companies won't need to snoop into your consumer preferences. As I described in my chapter on marketing, they'll be able to force you to buy whatever they're selling. Companies only ask one question: Does this person still have money left? Privacy will not be an issue.

Criminals invade your privacy to get your secret banking codes so they can steal your money. Sophisticated systems will be developed to thwart them. You will someday have to submit a urine sample at your ATM and wait for the results of an instant DNA analysis before you can get cash. You won't like it at first, but you'll get used to it. In fact, it might have some hidden benefits.

PREDICTION 58

In the future, you'll hear the phrase, "I'll be right back.
I gotta take a wicked withdrawal."

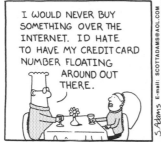
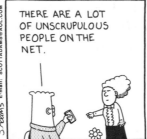
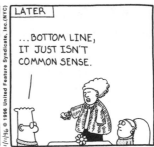

Sometimes people invade other people's privacy to get cheap thrills, but imagine a future where it's easy to snoop on anyone doing anything anyplace. It would quickly lose its thrill. We know this by examining other cultures.

In my many travels across my living room to the couch to watch *National Geographic* specials, I have noticed that women in some regions of the world go topless all day long. This does not excite the local men, because they are used to it. But if you dropped a nineteen-year-old male from another culture into the middle of that situation, he would quickly get a humiliating tribal nickname such as "one who constantly points the way forward." Over time he would get used to all the nudity and start fantasizing about women who wear thick jackets. I know this is true, because halfway through the *National Geographic* specials, I'm doing the same thing and I'm perfectly normal.

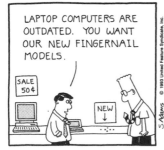
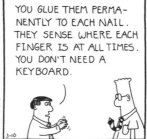
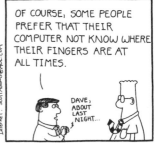

PET SERVICES

In the future, people will spend much more money on their pets and relatively less money on other people. That's because people will realize, as I have, that humans are no more interesting than most house pets, and at least an animal will let you pet it without suing you.

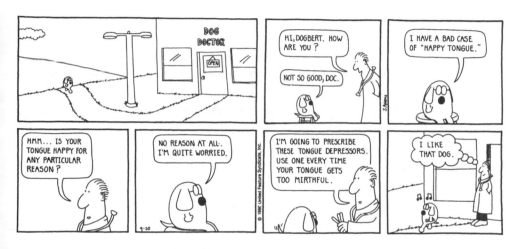

People, as I've explained so eloquently, are horny, stupid, and selfish. Pets are only stupid and selfish, assuming you have them fixed so they can't get horny. Therefore, mathematically speaking, pets are one-third superior to most of the people I know. And frankly, on average they're smarter than many of the Induhviduals I know, especially if you include dolphins in the calculation.

I realize this is an "apples-to-oranges" comparison, because you could have your friends fixed, too. Then they'd be almost as good as pets. But if your friends are like mine, they'll fight you every step of the way and not shut up about it until they're in the car on the way home.

The biggest problem with pet ownership is all of the regular scheduled maintenance. I have a big pile of postcards from my veterinarian reminding me of all the maintenance my cat needs—things you wouldn't know you needed unless someone told you:

- Urinary tract limpholeema.

- Feline diabolical emphlatemi shots.

- Tail stiffener serum.

- Braces.

I'm starting to think my vet is inventing things just to take my money. But I love my cats too much to take a chance, so Freddie goes in tomorrow for something called a petownerwalletectomy, which I understand will set me back a few grand.

This situation opens up a huge market for the future, a market that clever entrepreneurs are sure to fill: low-cost, efficient pet maintenance. Let's call it Jiffy-Pet™.

PREDICTION 59

In the future, there will be drive-through pet-care facilities.

The way a Jiffy-Pet would work is similar to the way specialty oil-changing services work. You'd tie your cat to the hood of your car like a hood ornament and drive into the Jiffy-Cat service bay. Once inside, a uniformed person who speaks too loudly would come out with a clipboard and explain what specials they are running that day.

Jiffy-Cat person: We've got a special on Catlube 6000.

Customer: What's that?

Jiffy-Cat person: Ooh, you need that if you want your cat to last another 10,000 miles.

Customer:	What's it do?
Jiffy-Cat person:	Okay, I see where you're coming from. Maybe you should just initial this box that says you don't love your cat.
Customer:	NOOOO! I LOVE my cat! Please give me some Catlube 6000!
Jiffy-Cat person:	Very good. Should I check her fluid levels?

Financially, this will be very similar to what you spend now at your veterinarian, but it will be more efficient. And you'll probably get a free car wash with every visit. (It will be a good idea to take the cat off the hood first.)

FOOD IN THE FUTURE

Take this quiz to find out if you are destined to become a crabby, dried-up old bag of twigs who dies young.

The thing I care most about is:

1. My body—the gift from God that allows my soul to strive for its highest potential during this brief mortal existence.

2. My automobile.

Generally speaking, people provide better maintenance for their cars than for their own bodies. Think about it. I don't know anyone who ever said, "My car needs oil, but I'm in a hurry so I'll just squirt some toothpaste in there and see if the oil warning light turns off." You wouldn't do that, because it would be bad for the car. Yet I know many people who would say, "I'm hungry. I think I'll have some bacon."

I know what you're thinking. You're thinking I'm one of those wise-ass

California vegetarians who is going to tell you that eating a few strips of bacon is bad for your health. I'm not. I say it's a free country and you should be able to kill yourself at any rate you choose, as long as your cold dead body is not blocking my driveway. I'm only addressing the question of how people pick priorities. Clearly, our automobiles are a higher priority than our bodies, because we take better care of them. But it's not entirely our fault. I blame the food industry.

The oil industry does it right. They make it easy to give our cars the right kind of oil. They refined the crude oil and added just the right combination of chemicals to make it the best oil it could be. It even has little detergents in there for people who are too lazy to clean the inside of their engines after every trip. Engine oil is a well-conceived product.

Why can't the food companies be like the oil companies? If I want to get the exact right combination of food nutrients, I have to bring a supercomputer and a team of scientists to the grocery store with me. And you know that wouldn't work if you've ever taken a team of scientists to the grocery store. They head straight for the Boboli pizza crusts and start tossing them around. Then one of the stocking clerks yells, "THOSE ARE NOT FRISBEES!" The scientists get kicked out of the store and you're stuck with this huge supercomputer and nobody to help run it.

You could ask one of the bag girls to help you run the supercomputer. They might even agree. But I wouldn't get my hopes up, because they aren't even sincere when they ask if you'd like help getting your groceries to the car. In fact, it sounds a little sarcastic when they say it to me. That's why I usually roll up my sleeves, strike a pose, and yell, "Look at those guns! Does it look like I need HELP?"

So I'm on my own when it comes to nutrition. I have a vague idea what foods are "good for me," but how do I know how much of each thing to eat? Clearly, it's important to get the right mix on a regular basis.

Today I ate twelve Snickers bars (the little ones), half a bag of potato chips, a banana, and a bunch of Spanish peanuts. I watered it all down with a cup of coffee and three diet Cokes. Later, I had two bites of a canned pineapple so I wouldn't get scurvy. And the pathetic part of this (if

I can single out one thing) is, "I ACTUALLY CARE ABOUT WHAT I EAT!"

I read a diet book called *The Zone*. Actually, I skimmed it, which is like reading except without the comprehension. Now I consider myself on *The Zone* diet, in the sense that I tend to eat whatever is in the zone of my kitchen when I'm hungry. So far I've lost ten pounds, but mostly muscle. (I'm hoping someone will find my lost muscles and return them to me, because I don't think I can ask for help carrying my grocery bags at this point.)

It's just too hard to eat right. Imagine if the oil companies acted like grocery stores. They'd give you a barrel of crude oil and several bottles of chemicals and tell you to mix it all up yourself. They wouldn't tell you how much of each chemical to use. Instead, they'd give you a government pamphlet with a pyramid showing oil at the bottom and detergent at the top. You'd be on your own to work out the specifics.

PREDICTION 60

In the future, you will not need a supercomputer and a team of scientists in order to get good nutrition.

Someday, you will be able to buy a burrito-like meal that is engineered as scientifically as a can of motor oil. This burrito-like thing will have just the right combination of food to give you 100 percent of what your body needs. It won't require much invention, just combinations of existing foods and some clever packaging.

Imagine the impact on health if people had a convenient way to eat healthy food. If better eating habits could cut health costs by 10 percent— and that's a modest goal—the impact on the economy would be gigantic. Assuming it's cheap (healthy foods tend to be inexpensive), it could be the most economical way to deal with poverty without raising taxes.

If someone doesn't build this burrito thing (or maybe it's a souplike thing), then I'll build it myself. Someone is going to make a trillion dollars selling low-cost, nutritious meals to Induhviduals, and it might as well be me.

First, I'm going down to my kitchen zone and eat a big bag of potato chips for dinner. I wish I were kidding.

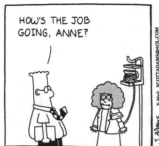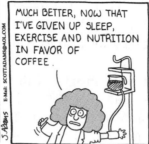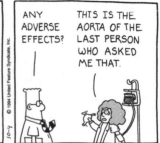

TWELVE

ENDANGERED SPECIES

I have whale guilt. I don't mean I feel guilty that the whales are an endangered species, I mean I feel guilty that I don't care as much as I should.

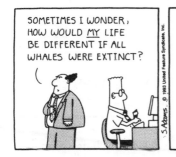
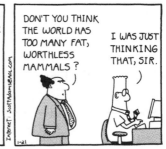

SOMETIMES I WONDER, HOW WOULD _MY_ LIFE BE DIFFERENT IF ALL WHALES WERE EXTINCT?

IT'S NOT LIKE THEY DO ANYTHING FOR US. YOU NEVER HEAR OF SEEING-EYE WHALES. THEY CAN'T FETCH THE PAPER OR DRAG YOU OUT OF A BURNING BUILDING...

DON'T YOU THINK THE WORLD HAS TOO MANY FAT, WORTHLESS MAMMALS?

I WAS JUST THINKING THAT, SIR.

Whales don't have much impact on my life. Whenever I'm removing a staple from a document, I do not say to myself, "This would go much easier if I had a whale." A staple remover works just fine. In a pinch, a fingernail will do.

When I'm lonely, I never say, "If only I had a whale to keep me company." I have television to fill that void. A whale would just ruin my carpet.

I might feel different if I'd ever seen a whale in person. I tried to see a whale once. In San Francisco, there's a boat that takes tourists out to spot whales. I went on the tour, but the closest I got was when someone on the other side of the boat yelled, "I SAW A TAIL." I raced over just in time to hear, "It's gone now."

This process repeated itself many times until I started getting into the spirit myself. I'd yell, "THERE'S ONE! AND IT'S WITH A BABY!" The other tourists would stampede to my side just in time to hear me say, "It was unbelievably cute. But they're gone now. It changed my life. Give me all of your addresses and I'll send you pictures."

It took a while for them to catch on. I think I lost my credibility when I yelled, "IT'S A GREAT WHITE! AND IT HAS THE CAPTAIN IN ITS MOUTH! AAAAHHHHHH!"

Now I'm banned for life from the whale-watching tours. But I'm not worried about seeing additional whales. I predict that in the future the problem will be too many whales, not too few, thanks to genetic engineering.

PREDICTION 61

In the future, there will be so many new kinds of whales, we'll all be sick of looking at them.

I think the scientists will be able to whip up any kind of whale we want in the lab and then release it in the bay, sewer, or anyplace else we think would look better with a few whales. And you won't have to make do with the boring gray and humpback whales we have now. We'll have polka-dot whales, two-headed whales, talking whales, whalephants, flying whales, you name it. I'm not saying this will be a good thing, but it will give us a whole new attitude about how many species are too many.

I JOINED THE "SPOTTED CHIPMUNK PRESERVATION SOCIETY."
S.Adams
E-Mail: SCOTTADAMS@AOL.COM
WE'RE GOING TO TRANQUILIZE THE LAST KNOWN MALE AND UNITE IT WITH A FEMALE.
THERE HE IS!
THUNK!
POW
1-30
© 1994 United Feature Syndicate, Inc.
WHEN YOU THINK ABOUT IT, THAT'S AN AWFULLY LARGE DART TO USE ON A CHIPMUNK.
IT'S DILBERT'S TURN TO WRITE THE NEWSLETTER.
TRUST ME. HUMOR IS THE WAY TO GO. IT EASES TENSION.
YEAH, BUT A WHOLE ISSUE OF DEAD CHIPMUNK JOKES?

SOME THINGS WON'T IMPROVE

Most things will improve in the future, but some things won't, because the designers who make those things prefer to keep them in their current sadistic form.

PREDICTION 62

Two things that will never improve in the future are
airlines and bicycle seats.

AIRLINES

In the future, airline travel will be just as uncomfortable as it is today. Airline comfort hasn't improved in my lifetime. There's no reason to think it will get better in the future. I was baffled by this lack of progress until I finally figured out why: Those jets last thirty years.

Jets cost millions of dollars, so you have to keep them until they plow into the side of a mountain. Airlines can't afford to throw out the old jets and buy new ones. Nor can they realistically have a fleet that is partly old uncomfortable planes and partly new comfortable planes. That would make people complain every time they flew in the old planes. So the obvious solution is to make new planes as uncomfortable as the old ones. That way nobody knows what they are missing. The newer jets have better fuel efficiency and safety features, but comfort-wise, they are the same as the old ones.

The thing that bothers me the most about the flying experience is checking in. I want someone to tell me what all the typing is about.

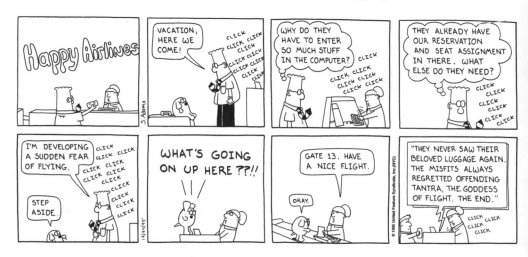

BICYCLE SEATS

Bicycle seats will never improve. The bicycle industry has apparently decided that the perfect design for a bicycle seat is a hard plastic object carefully engineered to avoid contact with the two padded portions of your buttocks.

It is very difficult for me to understand why my office chair can be designed to accommodate my entire bottom, but a bicycle seat cannot. Do the inventors of bicycle seats think their customers have magic buttocks that change shape when they exercise? I have no clue. But whatever the reason, it's not likely that bicycle seats will improve in the future.

GREAT SOLUTIONS IN ENGINEERING
S. Adams
E-Mail: SCOTTADAMS@AOL.COM
PROBLEM: BICYCLE SEATS ARE HARD. THEY HURT.
7-18
© 1994 United Feature Syndicate, Inc.
ANALYSIS: THERE MUST BE SOMETHING WRONG WITH YOUR PANTS.
SOLUTION: DORKY PANTS

A NEW VIEW OF THE FUTURE

Despite the fact that the future will be filled with an ever-growing number of idiots, I remain optimistic. This chapter will explain why I feel immune from their influence and why you might, too.

My explanation starts with a serious prediction that will make you shake your head, roll your eyes, and wonder what's gotten into me.

PREDICTION 63

The theory of evolution will be scientifically debunked in your lifetime.

The remainder of this book will be more bizarre and thought-provoking than whatever you expected. I'm turning the humor mode off for this chapter (except for the comics), because what you're going to read is so strange that you would be waiting for the punch line instead of following the point.

?
HOWDY!
I'VE NEVER SEEN A FISH WITH LEGS.
I'M EVOLVING INTO A HIGHER LIFE FORM.
THAT SOUNDS LIKE A LOT OF WORK.
YEAH... THE HARD PART IS FINDING A MATE WHO ISN'T TURNED OFF BY LEGS.
WITH ANY LUCK, THE KIDS WILL BE MUTANTS TOO.
I'M HOPING THEY'LL HAVE ARMS BUT NOT LOOK TOO MUCH LIKE RODNEY DANGERFIELD.
© 1991 United Feature Syndicate, Inc.
THESE LEGS ARE A NATURAL ADVANTAGE!
OH, THAT'S ORIGINAL.

I READ THAT DINOSAURS EVOLVED INTO THE BIRD FAMILY.
THAT'S EXACTLY CORRECT, DOGBERT.
© 1990 United Feature Syndicate, Inc.
BUT MOST PEOPLE DON'T REALIZE THAT THERE WAS A VERY DIFFICULT PERIOD WHEN SOME DINOSAURS STARTED EVOLVING INTO BIRDS.
"LEARNING TO FLY WAS THE HARDEST PART."
"AND LIVING IN TREES WAS A REAL NUISANCE."
BOY, THAT SOUNDS TOUGH.
THE TRAGIC PART IS THAT WE DID IT JUST FOR THE "BONUS MILES."

My prediction about evolution being debunked is part of a larger prediction. I believe that the next 100 years will bring about new ways of looking at existing things, as opposed to finding knew things to look at. It will be about perception and not vision.

PREDICTION 64

The next 100 years will be a search for better perception instead of better vision.

Most of human history has been an obsession to improve our visual understanding of our Universe. Almost everything we know is based on looking at things. We do experiments and we look at the results. We build microscopes to look at small things. We build telescopes to look at distant things. We build vehicles to take us where we can look at new territory. One of our most fundamental beliefs is that the things we see with our eyes are a good approximation of reality.

We use our other senses, too, but mostly we look at things and draw conclusions. That has worked well for most of human existence. But there have been some big-time blunders caused by looking at the world and using our brains to draw conclusions.

The most well-documented blunder caused by our vision was the historical belief that the Sun revolved around the Earth. It sure looks that way. Until an alternate theory was suggested, no other possibility was obvious. Here were the two biggest and most important objects in our field of vision—the Earth and the Sun—and virtually every person who looked at them got a totally backward perception of their movements.

People thought the Earth was flat because that's the only model that fit the way things looked. People didn't change their minds until someone took a boat and sailed out for a better look.

You might be tempted to say that these are isolated instances involving primitive times in our history, so it's not relevant to the future. But these isolated instances involved the biggest objects in our reality. These were not trivial misunderstandings. Our eyesight was inadequate for the task. It took some experimentation and a lot more looking to find the truth.

What if there are other optical illusions about our existence that are just as major as the illusion of the Sun revolving around the Earth? If so, how big are the opportunities that would emerge from a clearer perception?

What are the odds that you live in exactly the window of human existence when all of the major optical illusions have been discovered? Wouldn't that be an amazing coincidence, since every previous generation of humans has believed they were born in that window of time? They were all wrong, but they all thought they were right, just like we do now.

This is a hugely important question, because if your view of reality is flawed, then your strategies for succeeding are also probably flawed. If you change your assumptions, you have to change your plan.

For the rest of this chapter, I'm going to give you some mental exercises and scientific tidbits that might change your view of how much you understand about your reality. In so doing, I'll give you an alternate view of reality, one in which evolution makes no sense.

Don't worry, I won't be addressing the religious interpretations. There's nothing here that contradicts your religious beliefs, no matter what they are. I'll be talking about the limitations of eyesight as a source of knowledge, nothing more. I don't think the reality I'm going to describe here is the "right" one or the "only" one that could be described, but I think it's as logical as what I'll call the "normal" view.

It has been my experience that when I craft my strategies for success around this alternate reality, I get better results than when I assume reality conforms to the normal view. I realize that my personal experiences are not persuasive from a statistical perspective, but statistics mean nothing in my alternate view of reality (you'll see why). So neither perspective can be used to verify the other.

Are you getting curious yet or just confused?

I'm sure that some—if not all—of what I tell you next is scientifically inaccurate and maybe even illogical. It won't make any difference for my purpose. I'm just trying to help you imagine how your reality COULD be completely different from what you perceive and still LOOK exactly the way it looks. That alone will give you some freedom to try other approaches to success. Sometimes the first step to finding a better approach is to recognize the limitations of the current approach. That's as far as I can take you.

I'm not intentionally making up any facts in this chapter, but I'm not bright enough to get all of the scientific stuff exactly right either. Nor am I sufficiently interested in accuracy to spend a lot of time researching it. But if any of the points I make ring true, it will help you imagine a different world. That's all I'm aiming for. Read it with as many grains of salt as you need to be comfortable.

If you feel inspired to do so, I encourage you to research the scientific tidbits, think about the logic of it all, and tell me how uninformed and stupid I am. If that process makes you think about anything differently, this chapter did its job, regardless of where you come out.

In your normal view of reality, there are several things that seem unquestionably true. When I say "seem true," I mean that they look to be true from a visual perspective and you can't imagine any alternative. Here are some things I think you assume about reality.

Assumptions About Reality

1. Time goes forward.

2. Objects move.

3. Gravity exists.

4. A "cause" can only have an "effect" on something it physically contacts, directly or indirectly.

Obviously, if any one of those assumptions is wrong, your entire view of reality is totally, fundamentally, completely wrong. And so are your strategies for success. I'm going to cast some doubt on each of those assumptions, as unlikely as that might seem.

I can trace the beginnings of my own doubts about reality to a childhood friend named John. His family vacationed in my little town in upstate New York every summer. As a preteen, I spent hours with John and various members of his clan playing poker, Monopoly, and other games that required more luck than brains.

I never won.

John and his entire family boasted openly about their Irish luck. I can vouch for the fact that it seemed to defy statistical odds. To them, luck wasn't an abstract concept; it was palpable. They expected it and they got it with absurd regularity. If you spent much time with them, you got the impression that somehow they could make luck happen and they knew it.

One day his family and mine both visited a church charity event featuring booths with ring tosses, pop-gun shooting, and similar games of "skill." The games were designed to be unwinnable except by luck. My family dutifully complied, emptying our pockets in record time and having no prizes to show for it. But John's family had a different experience. I still have the image burned in my memory of John's mother making a special trip back to the car with an armload of impossible-to-win prizes. It was like a scene from a bad comedy. They weren't just winning, they were winning the things you aren't supposed to win no matter how lucky you are: cameras, telescopes, large stuffed animals. It was obscene. I believe they only stopped playing the games out of a sense of guilt.

The last time I saw John and his family was right after they found out they had won the grand prize in the Irish Sweepstakes—$120,000. This was the Sixties, so it was a much bigger pile of money than it seems today, and I believe it was the biggest prize of its kind in the world.

I realize that someone has to win the top prize, and I realize that statistics allow for clustering of unlikely events, but it was their expectation of luck that made me question my understanding of how the Universe was wired. It opened my mind to the possibility that luck can be managed.

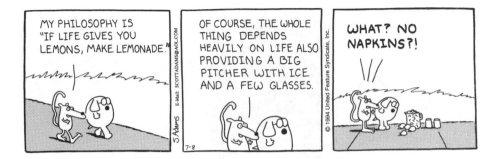

You probably don't know anyone like John and his family. I've never met any group like them before or since. But you probably know someone who expects to have *bad* luck and seems to consistently experience it. Think about that person right now and use that thought as a doorway to the rest of this chapter. You're about to take an interesting trip.

THE DOUBLE SLIT EXPERIMENT

I read about the double slit experiment in *Newsweek*. It's a well-known experiment among the physics crowd, and it's repeatable. I'll try to explain it in simple terms. You'll still have to read this section several times before you convince yourself you've read it correctly.

Here's how it works. You take a light source and shine it through a barrier that has two slits. Then you examine the light pattern on the surface behind the barrier. You would expect to see two bars of light corresponding to the slits, but you don't. You see multiple bars, like a venetian blind pattern.

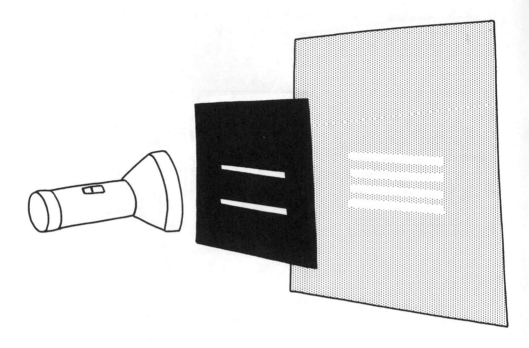

This nonobvious result interested the scientists who devised the experiment, so they hooked up some equipment that would record information about the light passing through the slits. When they recorded information about the light, they didn't get a venetian blind pattern anymore. They saw a blotch pattern instead.

You're probably thinking that the way they measured the light must have changed it. The scientists thought of that, too. So they did the experiment two ways, each time measuring the light the same way, but in one case the measured information was automatically erased after being measured.

When the information was automatically erased, the light pattern was a venetian blind, but when the information was *not* erased, the light pattern was a blotch.

The Scientists' Conclusion:

Information in the present can change the past.

Read that sentence again. I'll wait.

Let me say it another way, because I know it's hard to grasp. When the scientists had access to the recorded information about the light in the present, the light pattern in the past was a venetian blind, but when the scientists did *not* have access to the information in the present, the pattern in the past was a blotch.

It might seem impossible for you to conceive that time doesn't always march in one direction, bringing with it a perfectly ordered sequence of causes and effects, but it's not hard for me to imagine it, because I'm dyslexic.

When I hear a phone number spoken quickly, I hear all the numbers, but don't have any impression in what order they were spoken. It's as if they came in all at once. I have no problem imagining a reality where everything happens at once and some aspect of our perceptions straightens it all into an artificial sense of order. To me, disorder in the direction of time seems normal, at least some of the time.

Obviously, the brain is capable of perceiving time in an incorrect order. In fact, it happens all the time, even to nondyslexic people, but we don't acknowledge it.

In laboratory tests, it has been shown that sometimes the portion of the brain responsible for making a decision doesn't even activate until slightly after the action has been made. If I poke you in the butt with a pin, you jump before your conscious mind realizes what happened. But your immediate memory will be that you felt a poke and then moved. In this example, you would have perceived time backward, because what really happened is that you jumped from reflex and only afterward realized why.

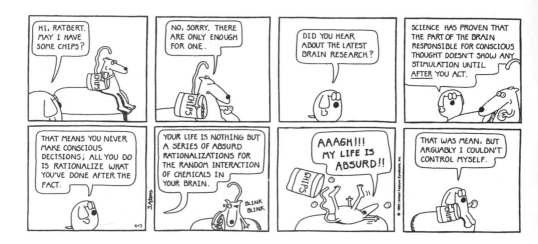

If brains can perceive time in any order, it raises the question of whether time is an independent thing or just a perception. Your perception of color might be a good analogy. Objects seem to have color, but, in fact, it's just a perception caused by the reflection of light. The color is a perception created by your mind. It is not a quality of the object.

Could time be in your mind and not in the environment? Time, like color, is something you can't put in a bottle. You can't get a handful of color or a handful of time. Most physicists have dispensed with the word altogether, preferring the phrase space-time, because it allows them to create a definition that's more useful for the physical world. I'm not sure what space-time means to physicists, but I'm sure it's different from my perception of the passage of time.

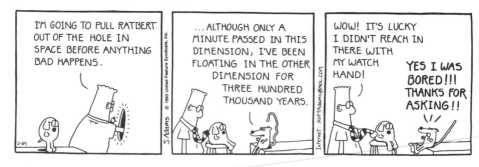

OBJECTS MOVE

Most people would agree that reality is full of objects that move around. Planets move, people move, molecules move. Everything is moving all the time.

What if all the motion we observe is an optical illusion? Let me paint a picture where you can imagine how nothing that appears to be moving actually moves, yet still looks like it does.

In cartoons, Bugs Bunny appears to be moving, but it's an illusion caused by lots of still frames being shown in sequence. Some physicists theorize that reality is like the frames of an animated movie, with infinite universes existing at once.

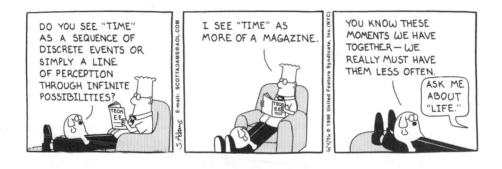

What if every possible universe existed simultaneously, each one only slightly different than its neighbor, like the frames of an animated movie? None of the universes in this model have movement. All the people and objects are frozen in one position. The only thing that moves in this reality is your perception (some might call it a soul), inhabiting one "you" after another in an endless string of nonmoving universes. Your perception would be that you were in one universe, but everything in it was moving. In fact, the only thing moving would be your line of perception from one "you" to another in each adjacent universe. And because each frozen universe is slightly different, your perception is that the things in it are moving.

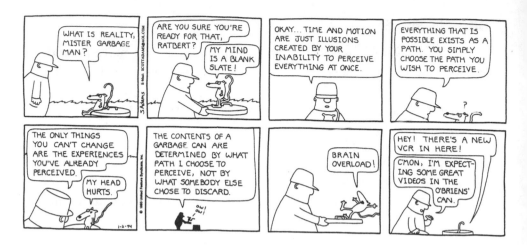

Have you ever pulled up to a stoplight next to a city bus? If you see the bus gradually moving out of the corner of your eye, you sometimes think incorrectly that your car is rolling in the opposite direction—because your field of reference is changing. You press your brakes frantically to stop it. In this case, your perception of motion is completely opposite from reality. The bus is moving, not you. Reality could be that way, too, and it would look just the way it looks to you now.

The view of reality I'm describing can't be proven, but it can't be disproved either. The same holds true for your current view of reality. It cannot be proven or disproved. Maybe there are lots of other models that would result in our current perception yet are quite different from what we assume.

GRAVITY EXISTS

It's hard to doubt that gravity exists. Every single thing you see appears to be affected by it. Gravity appears to be a force that reaches across space and somehow connects two objects, making them attracted to each other. That's what it looks like.

But scientists can't find gravity. They can only measure its effect. You can't fill a cup with gravity or block its effect with some sort of shield or find its molecules under a microscope. So where is it?

The best explanation that Einstein could come up with about gravity is that it was like a bowling ball on a bed—a heavy object bending the fabric of space. That explanation is virtually useless for a visual understanding. Physicists talk about gravity in terms of multiple dimensions, but we're not capable of seeing in more than three dimensions. It's safe to say that whatever we perceive about gravity—our simple model of objects being attracted—is an optical illusion.

To understand how gravity can look and act the way it does and be an optical illusion, let me describe a hypothetical universe. In this universe, there are only two objects: you and a huge planet-sized ball.

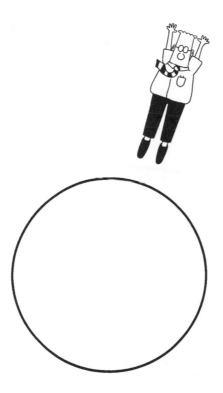

There is no gravity in this hypothetical reality in the classic sense of objects being attracted to each other. There is only one rule: Every piece of matter in this universe is constantly expanding, doubling in size every second.

You wouldn't notice the doubling, because both you and the huge ball would remain in the same proportion to each other. There would be no other reference points. And you wouldn't feel your own matter doubling any more than you feel the activity of the atoms in your body now.

In your current universe, you don't feel your skin cells dying, and you don't feel yourself being propelled at high velocity around the Sun or spinning with the Earth's rotation. So it shouldn't be hard to imagine how you could be doubling in size every second without being aware of it in the hypothetical universe.

The only effect you would feel from this doubling in size is the illusion of gravity. The ball's growth would cause a constant pushing against you. If you tried to "jump" away from the growing ball, you would create some space temporarily, but the ball's growth would catch up with you and close the distance quickly. To you, it would feel as though you were attracted to the huge ball and whenever you jumped "up," you would be sucked back down to it. There would be no gravity, but it would look and feel exactly like gravity.

Visually, it would seem that the huge ball had more "gravitational pull" than you do, because you seem to be attracted to it and not the other way around. This corresponds to our classic view of gravity—that huge objects have more of it.

Imagine a marble and a bowling ball. Now imagine they both instantly double in size. The marble still looks pretty much like a marble, but the bowling ball appears huge. When a large object doubles in size, it seems to have a disproportionately significant impact compared to a smaller object. So if gravity is an optical illusion, large objects would appear to create more of the illusion than smaller objects. That's consistent with what we see.

Now let's move from the hypothetical universe to our current universe filled with planets and other matter. You'd have to add another rule in order for the expanding matter theory to replace gravity in the current universe. You'd have to have a universe where all the major planets are moving away from each other quickly, otherwise they'd grow until they all bumped together.

In fact, the current universe does appear to be expanding, so that's no obstacle to the expanding matter theory. I can't think of anything in the "real" universe that would contradict the notion of gravity being an illusion caused by expanding matter. I'm not suggesting the theory is correct, only that it's a good mental exercise for seeing how things could be very different than you imagine them and still look the same.

The expanding matter theory came to me at 3:00 A.M. one day. I woke suddenly and sat straight up in bed with the idea fully formed in my head. I don't remember if it was inspired by a dream. At first, I thought it was either brilliant or totally stupid. I still don't know which it is. I first floated the idea in my *Dilbert Newsletter*, knowing that a million people would read it and some of them would surely write to tell me how stupid the idea was. I wrote it up as a whimsical theory from my cat Freddie, thus putting the blame on him. To my surprise, I received no reasonable criticisms of the theory. Instead, I heard a story about one physicist who had seriously pursued the same theory years ago, with no luck whatsoever, since there is no way to prove it experimentally.

I also heard that the theory was the subject of at least one science fiction book, although I'm not sure which one. So it's not a new idea. It's just an interesting one.

CAUSE AND EFFECT

You can't question the law of cause and effect, can you? When two things come in contact, they have an effect on each other. Logically, it's also true that if two things don't come in contact, they don't have any impact on each other.

The trouble is, how can you tell what things are really affecting other things and what are just optical illusions? Gravity seems to affect things at a distance. So do magnets. Yet there's no evidence that they touch.

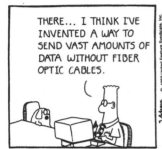 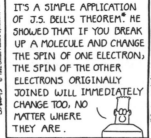 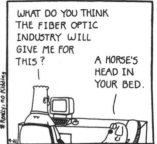

A physicist named John Stuart Bell performed a very strange experiment that was suggested by one of Einstein's theories. I'll simplify the explanation, probably getting the details wrong in the process, but you'll get the general idea.

You take a molecule and break it in half. If you change the rotation of the electrons on one of the halves, the electrons on the other half change at the same time. It doesn't matter how far apart the two halves are when you do it.

Whatever is happening in Bell's experiment defies our ability to understand it visually. Are the two halves of the molecule connected by some invisible force? Or is it an optical illusion and the two halves are never really separated? Or could one cause have two effects? We can't picture any of these explanations being correct.

Now consider the experiments that have been done to detect ESP. If you're a natural skeptic like me, you probably think there could be nothing flying through the air undetected that would allow ESP to work. Yet we read of experiments where some people seem to consistently beat the laws of averages in controlled ESP tests. Still, it seems impossible that ESP could be genuine. I am thoroughly unconvinced by media reports of *any-thing* unusual—much less ESP—because the media is so easily misled. This is the sort of thing I would have to experience firsthand in order to believe. And I have.

Years ago when I was taking a class to learn hypnosis, I met a woman who claimed to have psychic powers. I was highly amused by this concept and asked if I could hypnotize her so she could test her so-called powers in a trance. I'd heard reports that psychics are more accurate under hypnosis, so it was a good way to test my skills and also debunk the psychic for my amusement.

It didn't work out the way I planned.

I asked her to bring her deck of tarot cards. She did. We were in my home with no other people in a setting that I could totally control. I sat across the room from her and started the hypnosis. She slipped into a deep trance almost instantly. (There is anecdotal evidence that psychics are easily hypnotized. She certainly was.)

Then I shuffled her tarot cards and picked one. I asked her to describe what card I had in my hand. She described in detail the wrong card. My skepticism seemed justified. I picked another card and repeated the process, not telling her about her failure on the first. Again, she described the wrong card. But oddly enough, the wrong card she described was the first card I had picked. It was a coincidence, but still wrong. In all, I picked five cards, and she missed all five. Amazingly, the five cards she described were the five I picked, just out of order. I had been careful to keep them all close to my chest to remove any possibility that she was somehow peeking. And we were alone in my house, so no accomplices were involved.

I asked her why she guessed the cards out of order, and she explained that she can't distinguish between the near past and the near future. They are not relevant concepts to her. In her reality, the past and the present exist at the same time.

While still in a trance, and not in response to any question from me, she told me she saw a break in my aura. She traced her own body to show me where the break was in mine. Her hand stopped under one armpit. I was stunned.

I had a bad rash under that arm that I was having lots of trouble treating. It wasn't bad enough to cause itching or anything that would have tipped her off. We had no friends in common to feed her this information. Her information seemed to come out of nowhere. How lucky would you have to be to guess someone has a problem with one armpit?

Then, again without asking, she told me I was afraid of water. In fact, water is my *only* irrational fear. I have a healthy respect for many forms of danger, but only one truly irrational fear. And I've never known why.

Then she said, "And the reason is . . . "

At that point I was VERY interested, because I didn't know any reason I should fear water. Her credibility with me was growing by the moment. Suddenly, a picture formed in my head. It was a clear memory of an early childhood moment on a bridge with my parents. I was a toddler, and my father lifted me above the side railing so I could see a barge passing below. I remembered being filled with stark, blinding fear that somehow my father would lose his grip and I would fall into the water below the bridge.

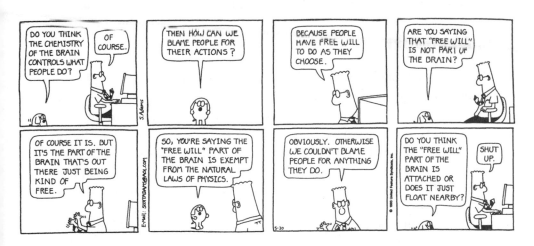

The moment the image filled my head, my psychic friend said, "I see a bridge."

As you can imagine, much of my skepticism disappeared at that point. She made many other predictions that night and in later conversations, most of them eerily accurate.

I don't expect you to believe the story about the psychic, although it's true. After all, I'm the media to you, and you should apply all due scrutiny when you hear a story like that one. But there might be an analogous situation in your own experience.

If you're a religious person, you believe that your body can be influenced by something nonphysical, specifically the soul. That would mean there is some connection between physical and nonphysical things, otherwise one could not influence the other.

Regardless of your personal experience or religious preferences, there's one thing we can agree on: Things in the Universe are connected in ways that we don't understand. It's certainly true with gravity, and it's true with the molecules in Bell's experiment. It seems plausible that if the Universe has connections that we can't see, then there are probably useful strategies for influencing the environment that we are not taking advantage of. I don't know if my psychic friend was taking advantage of some of these unseen connections or if souls do, but I no longer doubt it is possible.

CHAOS THEORY

What if our thoughts could influence the environment? It sounds ludicrously New Age–like to even consider the possibility, but when you think about the double slit experiment and how knowledge seems to influence the past, you begin to wonder how separate the mind and reality really are.

Even if you can't understand the invisible connections in our reality, maybe you can still use those connections. I can raise my arm simply by wanting it to happen, even though I have no idea how the thought is transformed into apparent motion.

What if your thoughts can influence things at a distance—but only in the tiniest ways—on the order of electrons, light particles, or even smaller? Could those tiny influences make any significant difference in your life?

According to chaos theory, the answer is yes.

Here again, I'm plunging into scientific waters way over my head, but I'll give you enough information so you'll get the basic idea. In chaos theory, you can show that the tiniest error in assumptions will cause any "complex iterative model" to give completely useless predictions.

An example of a complex iterative model would be a computer program for predicting the weather of the Earth. It's iterative in the sense that it calculates what each moment would be like and then uses that as a basis for calculating the next moment. Any tiny error in the first iteration would become compounded in the next, growing ever larger until the predictive ability of the program is useless.

Here's the classic explanation of chaos theory, which I'll borrow because it works so well: Suppose you had a weather model (a computer program) that could account for all the effects of wind, pressure, temperature, terrain, moisture, and sun. And suppose you fed the program with perfect information—except that you forgot to account for the impact of one butterfly beating its wings somewhere on Earth.

Chaos theory shows that your weather program would be effective at forecasting the weather tomorrow, because the butterfly effect is trivial on the first day. But over time, the omission of the butterfly causes each successive day's assumptions to be increasingly off. Eventually, the program will be completely useless. The nonobvious part of all this is how quickly and how hugely the tiny change can magnify itself. It defies visual logic.

Your life is a complex iterative model. Everything that happens today forms the basis for what can happen tomorrow. Infinitesimally small changes in your day today can magnify into huge changes over time. Every person who wins a lottery does so by the tiniest margin. The important people you meet could just as easily have been elsewhere that day. The virus you get, the memory you keep or lose, the inspiration you have—they all depend on the tiniest of electronic and chemical reactions.

We know that thoughts cause an electrical change in the environment outside your head. Scientists can put sensors on your scalp and detect slight changes in electrical impulses that correspond to your thoughts. Could this tiny change in electricity—barely detectable by sensors on your head—cause larger changes than our vision and common sense would allow us to believe?

If your thoughts can influence the environment—and there's circumstantial evidence that it can happen—can it happen in a planned way? Or is it all just random?

Suppose there really are an infinite number of motionless universes as I described earlier, and only your perception moves from one to the next. Can you steer your perceptions toward realities that are more to your liking?

AFFIRMATIONS

If it's possible to control your environment through your thoughts or steer your perceptions (or soul if you prefer) through other universes, I'll bet the secret to doing that is a process called "affirmations."

I first heard of this technique from a friend who had read a book on the topic. I don't recall the name of the book, so I apologize to the author for not mentioning it. My information came to me secondhand. I only mention it here because it formed my personal experience.

The process as it was described to me involved visualizing what you want and writing it down fifteen times in a row, once a day, until you obtain the thing you visualized.

The suggested form would be something like this:

"I, Scott Adams, will win a Pulitzer Prize."

The thing that caught my attention is that the process doesn't require any faith or positive thinking to work. Even more interesting was the suggestion that this technique would influence your environment directly and not just make you more focused on your goal. It was alleged that you would experience what seemed to be amazing coincidences when using the technique. These coincidences would be things seemingly beyond your control and totally independent of your efforts (at least from a visual view of reality).

The book also suggested picking a goal that you knew wouldn't happen by your extra effort alone. The author said you would never know if the affirmations worked unless you chose a highly unlikely goal.

So I tried affirmations. I figured it didn't cost anything so I had nothing to lose. My friend said it worked for her, coincidences and all, so I had a testimonial that sounded credible. It wasn't proof, but it was better than no testimonial at all. I picked what I thought was a very unlikely goal and went at it.

Within a week, coincidences started to happen to me, too. Amazing coincidences. Strings of them. I won't mention the specific goal I was working on, as it was a private matter, but within a few months the goal was accomplished exactly as I had written it.

I wasn't convinced the affirmations helped. Coincidences do happen on their own. And after all, maybe I had made some of my own luck. I considered the test inconclusive.

So I picked another goal—to get rich in the stock market. I wrote my affirmation down every day and waited for an inspiration. One day it happened. At about 4:00 A.M., my eyes snapped open, I awoke from a sound sleep, sat bolt upright in bed, and discovered the words "buy Chrysler" repeating in my head. (This kind of thing happens to me occasionally—the part about waking suddenly with a strange thought.)

At the time, this seemed like a very dumb thing to have in my head. It was during Chrysler's most bleak period. The company had only survived because of government loans. The stock was in a deep hole. (I forget the exact year, but if you've learned anything from this book, it's that I don't do research to get facts straight.)

Thinking that "buy Chrysler" was my inspiration, unlikely as it seemed, I quickly called a discount brokerage service to set up an account and buy some Chrysler stock. (Obviously, I didn't need a full-service broker, because I was getting all the advice I needed from the voices in my head.)

It took about two weeks to get the brokerage account established because of mail delays. During those two weeks, Chrysler stock climbed substantially. I figured I missed the window for buying it and cursed myself for not having a brokerage account set up in advance. Then a funny thing happened. Chrysler's stock kept growing. The company paid off its government loans earlier than anyone expected and went on a rampage. That year, Chrysler was arguably the best stock you could have owned.

I don't know how many stocks there are in the world, but it seemed awfully odd that during the time I was doing affirmations I woke up somehow knowing one of the best ones to buy. I wished I had followed my own advice.

So I tried again, this time promising myself I would follow my own inspiration no matter how flimsy and stupid it seemed. I wrote the affirmations and waited. Then one day I woke up somehow knowing that this was "the day." I picked up the newspaper and opened it knowing I was going to find my stock to buy. And there it was—a large announcement that a company called ASK was going public. I didn't know what their product was, except that it involved software. And I didn't care. This was my stock. I dialed my broker and bought $1,000 worth, which was the majority of my net worth at the time.

The stock climbed 10 percent almost immediately. Realizing that I was a brilliant investor, and wishing to lock in my gains, I sold after holding the stock only a few days. I pocketed a clean fifty bucks after taxes and commissions. I felt like a Rockefeller. Clearly, this affirmation technique worked.

Then a funny thing happened. ASK stock kept climbing. The media discovered it and wrote glowing assessments of its potential. It went on a rampage. That year, ASK was one of the best stocks you could have owned.

I don't know how many stocks there are in the world, but the odds of one idiot picking Chrysler and then ASK during that period were exceedingly small, especially if you take into account my sophisticated stock-picking methods.

I decided to unleash my affirmations on another goal that I had long since abandoned. I wanted to get my MBA from the University of California at Berkeley. They had the best evening MBA program within driving distance, and I needed that degree to become the business tycoon I always wanted to be.

The trouble was, I had already taken the GMAT exam several years before—it's a requirement for most MBA programs—and I earned a meager seventy-seventh percentile score. That wasn't good enough for Berkeley. It wasn't even close. I knew I had to be above the ninetieth percentile to have a chance.

I picked the ninety-fourth percentile as my specific outlandish target. My friend who told me about affirmations said I should be as specific as possible. I visualized the ninety-four exactly as it would appear on the results form, which was easy, because I'd seen the results form after my first GMAT.

I bought GMAT study books and took GMAT practice exams in the books for weeks before the actual test, each time scoring at about the seventy-seventh percentile. The experts say you can't improve your score dramatically by practicing, and I was proving them right. Hitting the ninety-fourth percentile was certainly going to be a stretch.

The day of the GMAT came. It felt just like the practice tests, no harder and no easier. Afterward, I kept up the visualization and the affirmations as I waited for the results in the mail.

I remember the moment I took the results envelope out of my mailbox. My heart was pounding. My future was in that envelope. I opened it and focused my eyes on the box that I had visualized a thousand times before. It was a ninety-four.

I looked again, certain I had misread it. It was still a ninety-four. I took it inside and looked again. Still ninety-four.

That evening, I sat in a chair with the GMAT results next to me, alternately staring at the wall and then staring at the ninety-four. I kept expecting it to change. It didn't. And that night I knew that nothing would ever be the same for me. Everything I thought I knew about how the Universe was wired was wrong.

I used the affirmations again many times, each time with unlikely success. So much so that by 1988, when I decided I wanted to become a famous syndicated cartoonist, it actually felt like a modest goal.

The odds of becoming a successful syndicated cartoonist are about 10,000 to 1. I knew the odds, but I figured they didn't apply to me. When I submitted my samples by mail to the major cartoon syndicates, I had a feeling of being exactly where I needed to be and doing exactly what I needed to do. I never once doubted it would work out the way it has.

Reporters often ask me if I am amazed at the success of the *Dilbert* comic strip. I definitely would be amazed, if not for my bizarre experiences with affirmations. As it was, I expected it.

I wasn't satisfied that *Dilbert* allowed me to make a comfortable living. I turned my affirmations toward making it the most successful comic on the planet. I figured that was another 10,000 to 1 shot. But as before, I figured the odds didn't apply to me.

It's hard to define what is "most successful" with comics. Everyone has their favorite. You can't really rank art or humor objectively. I took a pragmatic approach and decided the best measure was the number of *Dilbert* books sold. My reasoning was that people have to make a genuine choice with their own money when they buy a book, whereas you have no real influence over what runs in the newspaper. And as far as the "quality" of the strip, I decided the market could sort that out in book sales. If people liked the quality, they'd buy the book.

In June of 1996, *The Dilbert Principle* hit the number-one spot on the hardcover nonfiction list of the *New York Times*. It stayed in the top three all summer. In November, it was joined by *Dogbert's Top Secret Management Handbook*, giving me the number-one and number-two positions simultaneously for one week. For that brief period of time, *Dilbert* was the "most successful" comic on the planet, according to the limited definition I had set for it.

I don't know if there is one universe or many. If there are many, I don't know for certain that you can choose your path. And if you can choose your path, I don't know that affirmations are necessarily the way to do it. But I do know this: When I act as though affirmations can steer me, I consistently get good results.

I know that I have a better outlook on life when I think of reality in terms of infinite universes. When I think back to my GMAT results, I believe the contents of the envelope were variable until the moment I perceived what was inside. (For physics buffs, read about the Schrödinger's cat experiment to see how reality might actually exist in more than one state.)

In a world with infinite universes, there are infinite chances to get what you want, as well as infinite chances not to. If affirmations help you steer, maybe your odds are a matter of your control.

Several years ago, after having considerable success with affirmations, I developed a large lump on my neck. When the X rays came back, the cancer expert told me it was "probably" cancer. If it wasn't, he couldn't think of anything else it could be. But sometimes these lumps turn out to be, in his words, "just one of those things that go away." To me, the envelope wasn't open yet. Not until the biopsy.

I had a week to think about it. It's the kind of week you don't forget. I knew that the needle would enter the lump and draw out a sample of its contents. If the sample was red (blood), it was cancer. If it was clear, it was just "one of those things." I decided it would be clear. The doctor was surprised when it came out clear. I wasn't.

I have heard that patients who are prayed for recover better than those who are not. The patients themselves are not aware which group is being prayed for and which is not. The tests are small and inconclusive, but when viewed in the context of this chapter, they make you scratch your head. Depending on your religious views, you could replace everything I've said about affirmations with prayer and it starts looking very similar. And in the discussion of multiple universes, you could replace "point of view" with "soul" and lose nothing in the discussion.

At the time of this writing, I got a new car. I've been obsessing over how long it would be before it got its first dent. The thought was constantly on my mind as I drove it. I imagined every other car to be a potential missile heading my way. It bothered me that I couldn't relax and enjoy this lovely vehicle. A nice gentleman put me out of my misery by plowing into the car while I was parked at the gas station for its first refill. Did I somehow cause this to happen?

My last three cars have gotten bruised in the first month I owned them and then never again. In each case, the cars were parked when it happened. When I worried about the cars getting hit, they got hit. When I didn't worry, they didn't get hit. Every day it gets harder for me to believe my thoughts are separate from my reality.

Other people have read media reports of my use of affirmations and tried it themselves. Many of them have told me it worked for them, too. I have no proof that it works for me and even less evidence that it worked for them, but I do know it doesn't cost you anything to try.

I started the chapter by predicting that evolution would be debunked in your lifetime. I think physicists will raise enough questions about the nature of the Universe that evolution will require a second look. For example, if time doesn't move forward, or if there is no cause and effect, evolution makes no sense as a concept. I don't know the specifics of how evolution will lose its appeal, but I feel it coming.

I doubt the physicists will find a universe that has much in common with one described by a cartoonist, but I think it's a safe bet that our new understanding will be remarkably different from our current one. And in that new understanding of the Universe, all rules are off.

This makes me optimistic.

It would be easy to feel helpless in a vision-based universe where you're surrounded by idiots. Their sheer numbers would guarantee that you can't escape their impact no matter how clever you are or how hard you work. But I predict that will change.

PREDICTION 65

In the future, science will gradually free us from the optical illusions
that restrict our view of reality.

We may not have the capacity to fully understand "true" reality—if
indeed there is one—but we can shed the popular view of reality, the one
that keeps us in a prison of statistical likelihood. When we open ourselves
to new possibilities, it allows us to try new strategies.

Figuratively speaking, the year 2000 could very well be the "end of the
world" in terms of our outdated vision-based understanding of it. I think it
will be the beginning of something better—a world where our intentions
define reality in a more direct way than we ever imagined possible.

Personally, I can't wait.

AFFIRMATIONS TECHNIQUE

This technique is essentially stolen from a book and an author that I would credit if I knew how. I wouldn't normally do this, except my personal story has a huge gap without it.

If anyone can point me toward original work in this area, I will try to make that information available and give credit where it is due.

How to Do Affirmations

1. Have a specific goal, one that you can visualize.

2. Write it down fifteen times in a row, once a day, using the form:

"I, SCOTT ADAMS, WILL GET/DO/ACCOMPLISH WHATEVER."

3. There's no set time to expect results, but if I did it for six months without any movement toward the objective, I'd assume it doesn't work and I'd stop.

4. I don't think it matters how many times you write it, if you have multiple goals, if you forget to write it for a week, or if you type it instead of writing it. I don't have any reason to believe the method is so fragile that those things matter.

5. I don't think you need faith in the affirmations in order for the process to work, any more than you need faith to steer your car.

I'm fairly certain you would get the same results if you wrote the affirmations while thinking the whole thing is a load of crap. Be as skeptical as you like.

Affirmation Pitfalls

The only affirmation mistake I've seen is a lack of clarity in the goal. One person told me he was writing the following affirmation every day and having no success:

"I, JOE BLOW, WANT TO BE A FAMOUS JAZZ MUSICIAN."

I told him that, in fact, his affirmation had already worked exactly as he wrote it—he "wanted" to be a famous jazz musician. The better form would have been:

"I, JOE BLOW, *WILL BE* A FAMOUS JAZZ MUSICIAN."

The second problem is that his name wasn't Joe Blow, just in case you wondered.

I would also caution against affirmations that have specific deadlines, such as "I will get promoted by the end of this month." There are lots of ways to get to your goal, so leave some wiggle room.

And I don't recommend affirmations on things that can only happen one way—such as winning the lottery. That's asking a lot of your ability to steer. Better to set goals that have many ways of being realized. In the case of the lottery, your real goal was probably wealth. There are lots of ways to get wealthy. Don't constrain yourself.

APPENDIX B

DISCLAIMERS OF ORIGINALITY

I don't read many books. There are a lot of ideas floating around that I haven't been exposed to. Many of you will see ideas in this book that you'll be sure I stole from another author (beyond the ones I mentioned). It happens with my cartoon strip all the time. People write and say things like, "It's obvious from today's strip that you're reading J. P. Ferstershweizen's book *The Algonquin Paradigm*." To which I say, "Huh?"

Sometimes there are things I write or draw that are lifted from other authors, but it's usually subconscious. All authors do that. If I know I'm being influenced by an idea, I can generally change it enough to disguise it. My genuine thefts tend to go undetected. At my level of visibility, it would be dumb to plagiarize intentionally. In the vast majority of the cases where you see a distinct similarity between my work and someone else's, it's a coincidence involving an idea that wasn't all that creative to begin with.

I've witnessed at least a dozen people invent the phrase "roadkill on the information superhighway." They were all being "original" in the sense that they hadn't heard it someplace before. But it's an obvious idea.

I once thought I invented the idea of combining a Laundromat with a bar so single people could meet while doing laundry. I've met lots of people who think they invented that idea, too. And since the day I "invented" the idea, I've seen a number of news stories about entrepreneurs who have actually built such a business. In retrospect, it was an obvious idea. But sometimes it's not obvious which ideas will be obvious to someone else.

One day I drew a *Dilbert* cartoon about an opera singer who was an impostor. I referred to him as the "Placebo Domingo." I was very proud of that pun. That same afternoon, I opened my local newspaper and saw the exact same pun in another cartoon. Mine hadn't even been inked yet. If my cartoon had been published, the other cartoonist would have been suspicious that I lifted it from him. I threw mine away and drew another.

While I was writing my section in this book about video surveillance cameras being everywhere, I took a break and turned on *Oprah*. It was a show about how there are hidden surveillance cameras everywhere. I've never written on that topic, and I've never seen a show about it. They both happened in the same one-hour period of my life.

These are strange coincidences, but they happen more often than you would think possible. It is unlikely that even one idea in this book is "original" in the sense that nobody ever had a similar thought.

There are a few analogies in the last chapter of this book that I've seen in other works; e.g., the description of color as a perception and the discussion of the Earth rotating around the Sun. There might be others. I borrow them because they are useful and reasonably obvious. And they aren't central to what I'm saying.

If you have any comments on this, send me an e-mail message at scottadams@aol.com.